Philo of Alexandria

'Questions and answers on Genesis Books I-III

'The Early Jewish writers Series'

This is a publication of:
New Apostolic Bible Covenant ®
"Nova Vulgate Foederis Apostolicam"
MMXII - MMXIX

ISBN: 978-0-244-19483-3
1st Edition June 2019

Book designer: Apostle Horn
Design cover and composition: Apostle Horn
Source cover photo: https://www.google.com/search?

Questions and answers on Genesis

Index:

Preface:

Philo of Alexandria (/ˈfaɪloʊ/; Greek: Φίλων, Philōn; Hebrew:ידידיה הכהן, Yedidia (Jedediah) HaCohen; c. 25 BCE – c. 50 CE), also called Philo **Judaeus,** was a Hellenistic Jewish philosopher who lived in Alexandria, in the Roman province of Egypt. Philo used philosophical allegory to attempt to fuse and harmonize Greek philosophy with Jewish philosophy. His method followed the practices of both Jewish exegesis and Stoic philosophy. His allegorical exegesis was important for several Christian Church Fathers, but he has barely any reception history within Rabbinic Judaism. He believed that literal interpretations of the Hebrew Bible would stifle humanity's view and perception of a God too complex and marvelous to be understood in literal human terms. Some scholars hold that his concept of the Logos as God's creative principle influenced early Christology. Other scholars, however, deny direct influence but say both Philo and Early Christianity borrow from a common source. The few biographical details known about Philo are found in his own works, especially in Legatio ad Gaium (Embassy to Gaius) of which only two of the original five volumes survive, and in Josephus.The only event in his life that can be decisively dated is his participation in the embassy to Rome in 40 CE. He represented the Alexandrian Jews before Roman Emperor Caligula because of civil strife between the Alexandrian Jewish and Greek communities. We find a brief reference to Philo by the 1st-century Jewish historian Josephus. In Antiquities of the Jews, Josephus tells of Philo's selection by the Alexandrian Jewish community as their principal representative before the Roman emperor Gaius Caligula. He says that Philo agreed to represent the Alexandrian Jews in regard to civil disorder that had developed between the Jews and the Greeks in Alexandria, Egypt. Josephus also tells us that Philo was skilled in philosophy, and that he was brother to an official called Alexander the alabarch. According to Josephus, Philo and the larger Jewish community refused to treat the emperor as a god, to erect statues in honor of the emperor, and to build altars and temples to the emperor. Josephus says Philo believed that God actively supported this refusal.

[source; https://en.wikipedia.org/wiki/Philo]

Questions and answers on Genesis Book I

(1) Why does Moses, revolving and considering the creation of the world, say: "This is the book of the generation of heaven and earth, when they were created?" (Genesis 2:4). The expression, "when they were created," indicates as it seems an indeterminate time not accurately described. But this argument will confute those authors who calculate a certain number of years reduced to one, from the time when it is possible that the world may have been created. And again, the expression: "This is the book of the generation," is as it were indicative of the book as it follows, which contains an account of the creation of the world; in which it is intimated that what has been related about the creation of the world is consistent with strict truth.

(2) What is the object of saying, "And God made every green herb of the field, before it was upon the earth, and every grass before it had sprung up?" (Genesis 2:5). He here by these expressions intimates in enigmatical language the incorporeal species; since the expression, "before it was upon the earth," indicates the arriving at perfection of every herb, and of all seeds and trees. But as to what he says, that "before it had sprung up upon the earth," he had made every green herb, and grass, et caetera, it is plain that the incorporeal species, as being indicative of the others, were created first, in accordance with intellectual nature, which those things which are upon the earth perceptible to the outward senses were to imitate.

(3) What is the meaning of saying: "A fountain went up from the earth, and watered all the face of the earth?" (Genesis 2:6). But here the question is how it could be that the whole earth was watered by one fountain, not only on account of its size, but also because of the inequality of the mountainous and champaign situations? Unless, indeed, just as the whole force of the king's cavalry is called "the horse," so the whole multitude of the veins of the earth which supply drinkable water, may perhaps be called the fountain, inasmuch as they all bubble up like a fountain. And that expression is peculiarly appropriate which says that the fountain watered, not the whole earth, but its face; as in the living being it waters the chief and predominant part (the mind or the countenance). Since that is the most important part of the earth which can be good and fertile and productive, and that is the part which stands in need of the nourishment of fountains.

(4) What is the man who was created? And how is that man distinguished who was made after the image of God? (Genesis 2:7). This man was created as perceptible to the senses, and in the similitude of a Being appreciable only by the intellect; but he who in respect of his form is intellectual and incorporeal, is the similitude of the archetypal model as to appearance, and he is the form of the principal character; but this is the word of God, the first beginning of all things, the original species or the archetypal idea, the first measure of the universe. Moreover, that man who was to be created as a vessel is formed by a potter, was formed out of dust and clay as far as his body was concerned; but he received his soul by God breathing the breath of life into his face, so that the temperament of his nature was combined of what was corruptible and of what was incorruptible. But the other man, he who is only so in form, is found to be unalloyed without any mixture proceeding from an invisible, simple, and transparent nature.

(5) Why is it said that God breathed into his face the breath of life? (Genesis 2:7). In the first place because life is the principal part of the body; for the rest was only made as a sort of foundation or pedestal, and then life was put upon it as a statue. Besides, the sense is the fountain of the animal form, and sense resides in the face. Secondly, man is created to be a partaker not only of a soul but also of a rational soul; and the head is the temple of the reason, as some writers have called it.

(6) Why is God said to have planted a Paradise? And for whom? And what is meant by a paradise? (Genesis 2:8). The word paradise, if taken literally, has no need of any particular explanation; for it means a place thickly crowded with every kind of tree; but symbolically taken, it means wisdom, intelligence both divine and human, and the proper comprehension of the causes of things; since it was proper, after the creation of the world, to establish a contemplative system of life, in order that man, by the sight of the world and of the things which are contained in it, might be able to attain to a correct notion of the praise due to the Father. And since it was not possible for him to behold nature herself, nor properly to praise the Creator of the universe without wisdom, therefore the Creator planted the outlines of it in the rational soul of the principal guide of man, namely the mind, as he planted trees in the paradise. And when we are told that in the middle was the tree of life, that means the knowledge not only of the creature, but also of the greater and supreme cause of the universe; for if any one is able to arrive at a certain comprehension of that, he will be fortunate and truly happy and immortal. Moreover, after the creation of the world human wisdom was created, as also after the creation of the world the Paradise was planted; and so the poets say that the chorus of musicians was established in order to praise the Creator and his works; as Plato says, that the Creator was the first and greatest of causes, and that the world was the most beautiful of all creatures.

(7) Why in Adin, or Eden, is God said to have planted the Paradise towards the east? (Genesis 2:8). This is said in the first place because the motion of the world proceeds from the rising of the sun to its setting. And it first exists in that quarter from which it is moved; secondly, because that part of the world which is in the region of the east is called the right side; and that which is in the region of the west is called the left side of the world. Moreover the poet bears witness to this, calling the birds from the east dexteras or right, and those on the west sinistras or left; {1}{he is referring here to Homer "Ye vagrants of the sky! your wings extend, / Or where the suns arise, or where descend; / To right, to left, unheeded take your way, / While I the dictates of high Heaven obey."} when he says, whether they go to the right to the day and to the sun, or whether they go to the left towards the dusky evening. But the name Eden, when rightly understood, is an indication of all kinds of delights, and joys, and pleasures; since all good things and all blessings derive their beginning from the place of the Lord. Thirdly, because wisdom itself is splendour and light.

(8) Why did God place man whom he had created in the Paradise, but not that man who is after his own image? (Genesis 2:15). Some persons have said, when they fancied that the Paradise was a garden, that because the man who was created was endowed with senses, therefore he naturally and properly proceeded into a sensible place; but the other man, who is made after God's own image, being appreciable only by the intellect, and invisible, had all the incorporeal species for his share; but I should rather say that the paradise was a symbol of wisdom, for that created man is a kind of mixture, as having been compounded of soul and body, having work to do by learning and discipline; desiring according to the law of philosophy that he may become happy; but he who is according to God's own image is in need of nothing, being by himself a hearer, and being taught by himself, and being found to be his own master by reason of his natural endowments.

(9) Why does Moses say that every tree in the Paradise was beautiful to look upon and good to eat? (Genesis 2:9). He says this because the virtue of trees is of a twofold nature, consisting in bearing leaves and fruit, one of which qualities is referred to the pleasing of the sight, the other to the gratification of the taste; but the word beautiful was not employed inappropriately. Indeed it is very proper that the plants should be always green and flourishing perpetually, as belonging to a divine Paradise, which as such must be everlasting; and it is fit too that they should never degenerate so as to lose their leaves. But of the fruit he says, not that it was beautiful, but that it was good, speaking in a very philosophical spirit; since men take food, not only because of the pleasure which it affords, but also because of its use; and use is the flowing forth and imparting of some good.

(10) What is meant by the tree of life, and why it was placed in the middle of the Paradise? (Genesis 2:9). Some people have believed that, if there were really plants of a corporeal and deadly nature, there are also some which are causes of life and immortality, because, they say, life and death are opposed to one another, and because some plants are ascertained to be unwholesome, therefore of necessity there must be others from which health may be derived. But what these are which are wholesome they know not; for generation, as the opinion of the wise has it, is the beginning of corruption. But perhaps we ought to look on these things as spoken in an allegorical sense; for some say the tree of life belongs to the earth, inasmuch as it is the earth which produces everything which is of use for life, whether it be the life of mankind or of any other animal; since God has appointed the situation in the centre for this plant, and the centre of the universe is the earth. There are others who assert that what is meant by the tree of life is the centre between the seven circles of heaven; but some affirm that it is the sun which is meant, as that is nearly in the centre, between the different planets, and is likewise the cause of the four seasons, and since it is owing to him that every thing which exists is called into existence. Others again understand by the tree of life the direction of the soul, for this it is which renders the sense nervous and solid, so as to produce actions corresponding to its nature, and to the community of the parts of the body. But whatever is in the middle is in a manner the primary cause and beginning of things, like the leader of a chorus. But still, the best and wisest authorities have considered that by the tree of life is indicated the best of all the virtues of man, piety, by which alone the mind attains to immortality.

(11) What is meant by the tree of the knowledge of good and evil? (Genesis 2:9). This indeed exhibits that meaning which is sought for in the letter of the Scriptures more clearly to the sight, as it bears a manifest allegory on the face of it. What is meant then under this figure is prudence, which is the comprehension of science, by which all things are known and distinguished from one another, whether they be good and beautiful, or bad and unseemly, or in short every sort of contrariety is discerned; since some things belong to the better class, and some to the worse. Therefore the wisdom which exists in this world is not in truth God himself, but the work of God; that it is which sees and thoroughly investigates every thing. But the wisdom which exists in man sees in an incorrect and mixed manner with somewhat darkened eyes; for it is found to be incompetent to see and comprehend clearly and without alloy each particular thing separately. Moreover, there is a kind of deception mingled with human wisdom; since very often there are some shadows found which hinder the eyes from contemplating a brilliant light; since what the eye is in the body, such also is the mind and wisdom in the soul.

(12) What the river is which proceeded out of Adin by which the Paradise is watered, and from which the four rivers proceed, the Phison, and the Gihon, and the Tigris, and the Euphrates? (Genesis 2:10). The sources of the Deglath and of the Arazania, that is to say of the Tigris and Euphrates, are said to arise in the mountains of Armenia; but there is no paradise there at this day, nor do both the sources of both these rivers remain there. Perhaps, therefore, we ought to consider that the real situation of the Paradise is in a place at a distance from this part of the world which we inhabit, and that it has a river running beneath the earth. which pours forth many veins of the largest size; so that they, rising up together, pour themselves forth into other veins, which receive them on account of their great size, and then those have been suppressed by the gulfs of the waves; on which account, through the impulse given to them by the violence which is implanted in them, they burst out on the face of the earth in other places, and also among others in the mountains of Armenia. Therefore, those things which have been accounted the sources of the rivers, are rather their flowing course; or again, they may be said to be correctly looked upon as sources, because by all means we must consider the holy scriptures infallible, which point out the fact of four rivers; for the river is the beginning, and not the spring. But perhaps this passage also contains an allegorical meaning; for the four rivers are the signs of four virtues: Phison being the sign of prudence, as deriving its name from parsimony; {2}{from pheidoμ, "parsimony."} and Gihon being the sign of sobriety, as having its employment in the regulation of meat and drink, and as restraining the appetites of the belly, and of those parts which are blow the belly, as being earthly; the Tigris again is the sign of fortitude, for this it is which regulates the raging commotion of anger within us; and the Euphrates is the sign of justice, since there is nothing in which the thoughts of men exult more than in justice.

(13) Why it is that he not only describes the situation of the Euphrates, but also says that the Phison goes round all the land of Evilat, and that the Gihon goes round all the land of Ethiopia, and that the Tigris goes toward Assyria? (Genesis 2:14). The Tigris is a very cruel and mischievous river, as the citizens of Babylon bear witness, and so do the magi, who have found it to be of a character quite different from the nature of other rivers; however they might also have another reason for looking on it with aversion. But the Euphrates is a gentler, and more salubrious, and more nourishing stream. On which account, the wise men of the Hebrews and Assyrians speak of it as one which increases and extends itself; and on this account it is not here characterised by its connection with other things, as the other three rivers are, but by itself. My own opinion is, that these expressions are all symbolical, for prudence is the virtue of the rational part of man; and it is in this that wickedness is sometimes found. And fortitude is that portion of the human character which is liable to degenerate into anger. And sobriety, again, may be impaired by the desires, but anger and concupiscence are the characteristics of beasts; therefore the sacred historian has here described those three rivers by the places which they flow round. But he has not described the Euphrates in that manner, as being the symbol of justice, for there is no certain and limited portion of it allotted to the soul, but a perfect harmony of the three parts of the soul and of the three virtues is possessed by it.

(14) Why God placed man in the Paradise with a twofold object, namely, that he might both till it and keep it, when the Paradise was in reality in need of no cultivation, because it was perfect in everything, as having been planted by God; nor, again, did it require a keeper, for who was there to ravage it? (Genesis 2:15). These are the two objects which a cultivation of the land must attain to and take care of, the cultivation of the land and the safe keeping of the things which are in it, otherwise it will be spoiled by laziness or else by devastation. But although the Paradise did not stand in need of these exertions, nevertheless it was proper that he who had the regulation and care of it committed to him, namely, the first man, should be as it were a sort of pattern and law to all workmen in future of everything which ought to be done by them. Moreover it was suitable that, though all the Paradise was full of everything, it should still leave the cultivator some grounds for care, and some means of displaying his industry; for instance, by digging around it, and tending it, and softening it, and digging trenches, and irrigating it by water; and it was needful to attend to its safety, although there was no one to lay it waste, because of the wild beasts, also more especially in respect of the air and water; as, for instance, when a drought prevailed, to irrigate it with a plenteous supply of water, and in moister weather to check the superabundance of moisture by directing the course of the streams in other directions.

(15) Why, when God commanded the man to eat of every tree within the Paradise, he speaks in the singular number, and says, "Thou shalt eat;" but when he commands that he shall abstain from the tree which would give him the knowledge of good and evil, he speaks in the plural number, and says, "Ye shall not eat of it, for in the day in which ye eat of it ye shall surely die?" (Genesis 2:16). In the first place he uses this language because one good was derived from many; and that also is not unimportant in these principles, since he who has done anything which is of utility is one, and he who attains to anything useful is also one; but when I say one, I am speaking not of that which in point of number comes before duality, but of that one creative virtue by which many beings rightly coalesce, and by their concord imitate singularity, as a flock, a herd, a troop, a chorus, an army, a nation, a tribe, a family, a state; for all these things being many members form one community, being united by affection as by a kiss; when things which are not combined, and which have no principle of union by reason of their duality and multitude, fall into different divisions, for duality is the beginning of discord. But two men living as if they were one, by the same philosophy, practise an unalloyed and brilliant virtue, which is free from all taint of wickedness; but where good and evil are mingled together the combination contains the principle of death.

(16) What is the meaning of the expression, "Ye shall surely die?" (Genesis 2:17). The death of the good is the beginning of another life; for life is a twofold thing, one life being in the body, corruptible; the other without the body, incorruptible. Therefore one wicked man surely dies the death, who while still breathing and among the living is in reality long since buried, so as to retain in himself no single spark of real life, which is perfect virtue. But a good man, who deserves so high a title, does not surely die, but has his life prolonged, and so attains to an eternal end.

(17) Why God says, "It is not good for man to be alone; let us make him a help meet for him?" (Genesis 2:18). By these words God intimates that there is to be a communion, not with all men, but with those who are willing to be assisted and in their turn to assist others, even though they may scarcely have any power to do so; since love consists not more in utility than in the harmonious concord of trustworthy and steadfast manners; so that every one who joins in a communion of love may be entitled to utter the expression of Pythagoras, "A friend is another I."

(18) Why, when God had already said, "Let us make a help for man," he creates beasts and cattle? (Genesis 2:19). Perhaps some gluttons and insatiably greedy persons may say that God did this because beasts and flying things were, as it were, necessary food for man, and his meetest helper; for that the eating of meat assists the belly so as to conduce to the health and vigour of the body. But I should think that by reason of the evil implanted in them by nature animals of all kinds, whether terrestrial or flying in the air, were in this age hostile to and contrary to man; but that in the case of the first man, as one adorned with every imaginable virtue, they were, as it were, allies, and a reinforcement in war, and familiar friends, as being tame and domestic by nature, and this was the sole principle of their familiarity with man, for this it was fit that servants should dwell with their lord.

(19) Why the creation of animals and flying creatures is mentioned a second time, when the account of their creation had already been given in the history of the six days? (Genesis 2:19). Perhaps those things which were created in the six days were incorporeal angels, indicated under these symbolical expressions, being the appearances of terrestrial and flying animals, but now they were produced in reality, being the copies of what had been created before, images perceptible by the outward senses of invisible models.

(20) Why did God bring every animal to man, that he might give them their names? (Genesis 2:19). He has here explained a great source of perplexity to the students of philosophy, admonishing them that names proceed from having been given, and not from nature; for a natural nomenclature is with peculiar fitness assigned to each creature when a man of wisdom and pre-eminent knowledge appears; and, in fact, the office of assigning the names to animals is one which particularly belongs to the mind of the wise man alone, and indeed to the first man born out of the earth, since it was fitting that the first of the human race, and the sovereign of all the animals born out of the earth, should have the dignity assigned to him. For inasmuch as he was the first person to see the animals, and as he was the first person who deserved to govern them all as their chief, so also it was fitting that he should be their first namer and the inventor of their names, since it would have been inconsistent and mad to leave them without any names, or to allow them to receive names from any one born at a later period, which would have been an insult to and a derogation from the honour and glory due to the first born. But we may also adopt this idea, that the giving of names to the different animals was so easily arranged that the very moment that Adam gave the name the animal itself also heard it; being influenced by the name thus given to it as by a familiar indication closely connected with it.

(21) Why does Moses say, "He brought the animals to Adam, that he might see what he would call them," when God can never entertain a doubt? (Genesis 2:19). It is in truth inconsistent with the nature of God to doubt; therefore it does not appear that he was in doubt on this occasion, but that since he had given intellect to man as being the first man born out of the earth and endowed with a great desire for virtue, by which he was made thoroughly wise as if he had been endowed with wisdom by nature, so as to consider all things like the proper Ruler and Lord of all, God now caused him to be influenced to display the proper performance of his task, and saw what was really the most excellent point of his mind. Besides this, by this statement he evidently indicates the perfect free-will existing in us, refuting those who affirm that everything exists by a certain necessity. Or else because it belonged to man to employ the animals, therefore he also gave him authority to give them names.

(22) What is the meaning of the expression, "And whatever he called each living thing, that was the name thereof?" (Genesis 2:19). We must consider that Adam gave names not only to all living creatures, but also to plants, and to everything else which is inanimate, beginning with the more excellent class; for the living creature is superior to that which has not life. Therefore the scripture considers the mention of the better part sufficient, indicating by this mention to all who are not utterly devoid of sense, that he in fact gave names to everything, since it was easy to fix names to things without life, which were never likely to change their place, and which had no passions of the soul to exercise, but the giving of proper appellations to living creatures was a more difficult task on account of the motions of their bodies and the various impulses of their souls, in accordance with the imagination and the variety of the outward senses, and the different agitations of the mind from which the effects of their works proceed. Therefore the mind could give names to the more difficult classes of living creatures. And on this account it was a very proper expression to employ, that he gave them names as being easy to name, because they were near.

(23) What is the meaning of the expression: "But for Adam there was not found a helper like to him?" (Genesis 2:20). Every thing was helping and assisting the prince of the human race: the earth, the rivers, the sea, the air, the light, the heaven. Moreover, every species of fruit and plant co-operated with him, and every herd of cattle, and every beast which was not savage. Nevertheless, of all these things which were assisting him, there was nothing like himself, inasmuch as they were none of them human beings. Therefore, God gave a certain indication that he might show that man ought to be an assistant to and co-operator with man, being endowed with perfect similarity to one another in both body and soul.

(24) What is the meaning of the statement, "And God sent a trance upon Adam, and caused him to sleep?" (Genesis 2:21). How it is that man sleeps is a question which has caused an extraordinary amount of perplexity to philosophers. But yet our prophet has distinctly explained this question; for sleep is in itself properly a trance, not of that kind which is more nearly allied to insanity, but of that which is in accordance with the dissolution of the senses and the absence of counsel; for then the senses withdraw from those things which are their proper object, and the intellect withdraws from the senses, not strengthening their nerves, nor giving any motion to those parts which have received the power of action, inasmuch as they are withdrawn from the objects perceptible by the outward senses.

(25) What the rib is which God took from the man whom he had formed out of the earth, and which he made into a woman? (Genesis 2:21 - 22). The letter of this statement is plain enough; for it is expressed according to a symbol of the part, a half of the whole, each party, the man and the woman, being as sections of nature co-equal for the production of that genus which is called man. But with respect to the mind, man is understood in a symbolical manner, and his one rib is virtue, proceeding from the senses; but woman, who is the sensation of counsel, will be more variable. But some think that the rib means valour and vigour, on which account men call a boxer who as strong loins eminently strong. Therefore, the lawgiver relates that the woman was formed out of the rib of the man, indicating by that expression, that one half of the body of the man is woman. And this is testified to by the formation of the body, by the way in which it is put together, by its motions and vigour, by the force of the soul, and its strength; for all things are regarded as in a twofold light; since, as the formation of the man is more perfect, and, if one may so say, more double than the formation of the woman, so also it required half the time, that is to say forty days; when, for the imperfect, and, if I may so call it, half section of the man, that is to say the woman, there was need of a double allowance, that is to say, of eighty days, so that the doubling of the time required for the nature of the man might be changed, in order to the formation of the peculiar properties of the woman; for that body, and that soul, the nature of which is in a twofold ratio, the body and soul, that is, of the man, require but half of the delineation and formation: but that body of which the nature and construction is in the ratio of one half, namely, that of the woman, her formation and delineation is in a twofold ratio.

(26) Why Moses calls the form of the woman a building? (Genesis 2:22).{3}{the margin of our Bible points out that the Hebrew word translated "made," means strictly "builded."} The union and plentitude of concord formed by the man and woman is symbolically called a house; but every thing is altogether imperfect and destitute of a home, which is deserted by a woman; for to the man the public affairs of the state are committed, but the particular affairs of the house belong to the woman; and a want of the woman will be the destruction of the house; but the actual presence of the woman shows the regulation of the house.

(27) Why, as other animals and as man also was made, the woman was not also made out of the earth, but out of the rib of the man? (Genesis 2:21). This was so ordained in the first place, in order that the woman might not be of equal dignity with the man. In the second place, that she might not be of equal age with him, but younger; since those who marry wives more advanced in years than themselves deserve blame, as having overturned the law of nature. Thirdly, the design of God was, that the husband should take care of his wife, as of a necessary part of himself; but that the woman should requite him in turn with service, as a portion of the universe. In the fourth place, he admonishes man by this enigmatical intimation, that he should take care of his wife as of his daughter; and he admonishes the woman that she should honour her husband as her father. And very rightly, since the woman changes her habitation, passing from her own offspring to her husband. On which account, it is altogether right and proper that he who has received should take upon himself the liability in respect of what has been given; and that she who has been removed should worthily give the same honour to her husband which she has previously given to her parents; for the husband receives his wife from her parents, as a deposit which is entrusted to him; and the woman receives her husband from the law.

(28) Why, when the man saw the woman who had been formed in this manner, he proceeded to say: "She" (for "this," touto) "is now bone of my bone and flesh of my flesh: she shall be called woman, because she has been taken out of man?" (Genesis 2:23).{4}{woman, virgo, or virago, is here looked upon as derived from vir, "man;" he also derives gyneμ from gennaoμ.} He might have been amazed at what he had seen, and have said in a negative manner: How can this exquisite and desirable beauty have been derived from bones and from flesh which are endowed with neither beauty nor elegance, being of a form so far more beautiful, and endowed with such excessive life and grace? The matter is incredible because she is like; and yet it is credible, because God himself has been her creator and painter. Again, he might have said affirmatively: Truly she is a living being, my bone and my flesh, for she exists by having been taken from that bone and flesh of mine. But he makes mention of his bone and flesh in a very natural manner; for the human or corporeal tabernacle is the combination of bones, and flesh, and entrails, and veins, and nerves, and ligaments, and blood-vessels, and breathing tubes, and blood. And she is called woman (in Greek gyneμ) with great correctness, as the power of producing with fertility, either because she becomes pregnant through the reception of the seed, and so brings forth; or, as the prophet says, because she was made out of man, not out of the earth, as he was; nor from seed, as all mankind after them; but of a certain intermediate nature; and like a branch, brought out of one vine to produce another vine.

(29) Why he says, "Therefore shall a man leave his father and his mother, and cleave to his wife, and they shall be two in one flesh?" (Genesis 2:24). He here orders man to behave himself towards his wife with such excess of affection in their intercourse, that he is willing to leave his parents, not in order that by that means it may be more suitable, but as they would scarcely be a motive for his fidelity to his wife. And we must remark, that it is very excellent and prudently done, that he has avoided saying that the woman is to leave her parents and cleave to her husband, since the character of the man is bolder than the nature of the woman; but he says that the man ought to do this for the sake of the woman; for he is borne on by a cheerful and willing impulse to the concord of knowledge, to which, becoming wholly devoted, he restrains and regulates his desires, and clings to his wife alone like bird-lime. Especially because he himself, delighting in his master-like authority, is to be respected for his pride: but the woman, being in the rank of a servant, is praised, for assenting to a life of communion. And when it is said that the two are one flesh, that indicates that the flesh is very tangible and fully endowed with outward senses, on which it depends to be afflicted with pain and delighted with pleasure, so that both the man and woman may derive pleasure and pain from the same sources, and may feel the same; aye, and may still more think the same.

(30) Why both of them, the man and the woman, are said to have been naked, and not to have been ashamed? (Genesis 2:25). They were not ashamed, in the first place, because they were in the neighbourhood of the world, and the different parts of the world are all naked, each of them indicating some peculiar qualities, and having peculiar coverings of their own. In the second place, on account of the sincerity and simplicity of their manners and of their natural disposition, which had not taint of pride about it. For ambition had as yet no existence. Thirdly, because the climate and the mildness of the atmosphere was a sufficient covering for them, so as to prevent either cold or heat from hurting them. In the fourth place, because they, by reason of the relationship existing between themselves and the world, could not receive injury from any part of it whatever, as being related to them.

(31) Why does Moses say that the serpent was more cunning than all the beasts of the field? (Genesis 3:1). One may probably affirm with truth that the serpent in reality is more cunning than any beast whatever. But the reason why he appears to me to be spoken of in these terms here is on account of the natural proneness of mankind to vice, of which he is the symbol. And by vice I mean concupiscence, inasmuch as those who are devoted to pleasure are more cunning, and are the inventors of stratagems and means by which to indulge their passions. Being, forsooth, very crafty in devising plans, both such as favour pleasure and also such as procure means of enjoying it. But it appears to me that since that animal, so superior in wisdom, was about to seduce man, it is not the whole race that is here meant to be spoken of as so exceedingly wise, but only that single serpent, for the reason above mentioned.

(32) Did the serpent speak with a human voice? (Genesis 3:2). In the first place, it may be the fact that at the beginning of the world even the other animals besides man were not entirely destitute of the power of articulate speech, but only that man excelled them in a greater fluency and perspicuity of speech and language. In the second place, when anything very marvellous requires to be done, God changes the subject natures by which he means to operate. Thirdly, because our soul is entirely filled with many errors, and rendered deaf to all words except in one or two languages to which it is accustomed; but the souls of those who were first created were rendered acute to thoroughly understand every voice of every kind, in order that they might be pure from evil and wholly unpolluted. Since we indeed are not endowed with senses in such perfection, for those which we have received are in some degree depraved, just as the construction of our bodies too is small; but the first created men, as they received bodies of vast size reaching to a gigantic height, must also of necessity have received more accurate senses, and, what is more excellent still, a power of examining into and hearing things in a philosophical manner. For some people think, and perhaps with some reason, that they were endowed with such eyes as enabled them to behold even those natures, and essences, and operations, which exist in heaven, as also ears by which they could comprehend every kind of voice and language.

(33) Why did the serpent accost the woman, and not the man? (Genesis 3:2). The serpent, having formed his estimate of virtue, devised a treacherous stratagem against them, for the sake of bringing mortality on them. But the woman was more accustomed to be deceived than the man. For his counsels as well as his body are of a masculine sort, and competent to disentangle the notions of seduction; but the mind of the woman is more effeminate, so that through her softness she easily yields and is easily caught by the persuasions of falsehood, which imitate the resemblance of truth. Since therefore, in his old age, the Serpent{5}{the ancients believed that the serpent became young again by casting his skin. Ovid says Anguibus exuitur tenui cum pelle vetustas.} strips himself of his scales from the top of his head to his tail, he, by his nakedness, reproaches man because he has exchanged death for immortality. His nature is renewed by the beast, and made to resemble every time. The woman, when she sees this, is deceived; when she ought rather to have looked upon him as an example, who, while showing his ingenuity towards her, was full of devices, but she was led to desire to acquire a life which should be free from old age, and from all decay.

(34) Why the serpent tells the woman lies, saying, "God has said, Ye shall not eat of every tree in the Paradise," when, on the contrary, what God really had said was, "Ye shall eat of every tree in the Paradise, except one?" (Genesis 3:4). It is the custom for contending arguers to speak falsely in an artful manner, in order to produce ignorance of the real facts, as was done in this case, since the man and woman had been commanded to eat of all the trees but one. But this insidious prompter of wickedness coming in, says that the order which they had received was that they should not eat of them all. He brought forward an ambiguous statement as a slippery stumbling-block to cause the soul to trip. For this expression, "Ye shall not eat of every tree," means in the first place either, not even of one, which is false; or, secondly, not of every one, as if he intended to say, there are some of which you may not eat, which is true. Therefore he asserts such a falsehood more explicitly.

(35) Why, when it was commanded them to avoid eating of one plant alone, the woman made also a further addition to this injunction, saying, "He said, Ye shall not eat of it, neither shall ye touch it?" (Genesis 3:3). In the first place she says this, because taste and every other sense after its kind consists in the touch appropriate to it. In the second place she says it that it may seem to condemn them themselves, who did what they had been forbidden. For if even the mere act of touching it was prohibited, how could they who, besides touching the tree, presumed to eat of the fruit, and so added a greater transgression to the lesser one, be anything but condemners and punishers of themselves?
(36) What is the meaning of the expression, "Ye shall be as gods, knowing good and evil?" (Genesis 3:5). Whence was it that the serpent found the plural word "gods," when there is only one true God, and when this is the first time that he names him? But perhaps this arises from there having been in him a certain prescient wisdom, by which he now declared the notion of the multitude of gods which was at a future time to prevail amongst men; and, perhaps, history now relates this correctly at its first being advanced not by any rational being, nor by any creature of the higher class, but as having derived its origin from the most virulent and vile of beasts and serpents, since other similar creatures lie hid under the earth, and their lurking places are in the holes and fissures of the earth. Moreover, it is the inseparable sign of a being endowed with reason to look upon God as essentially one being, but it is the mark of a beast to imagine that there are many gods, and these too devoid of reason, and who can scarcely be said with propriety to have any existence at all. Moreover, the devil proceeds with great art, speaking by the mouth of the serpent. For not only is there in the Divinity the knowledge of good and evil, but there is also an approval of what is good and a repudiation of what is evil; but he does not speak of either of these feelings because they were useful, but only suggested the mere knowledge of the two contrary things, namely, of good and evil. In the second place, the expression, "as gods," in the plural number, is in this place not used inconsiderately, but in order to give the idea of there being both a bad and a good God. And these are of a twofold quality. Therefore it is suitable to the notion of particular gods to have a knowledge of contrary things; but the Supreme Cause is above all others.
(37) Why the woman first touched the tree and ate of its fruit, and the man afterwards, receiving it from her? (Genesis 3:6). The words used first of all, by their own intrinsic force, assert that it was suitable that immortality and every good thing should be represented as under the power of the man, and death and every evil under that of the woman. But with reference to the mind, the woman, when understood symbolically, is sense, and the man is intellect. Moreover, the outward senses do of necessity touch those things which are perceptible by them; but it is through the medium of the outward senses that things are transmitted to the mind. For the outward senses are influenced by the objects which are presented to them; and the intellect by the outward

senses.

(38) What is the meaning of the expression, "And she gave it to her husband to eat with her?" (Genesis 3:6). What has been just said bears on this point also, since the time is nearly one and the same in which the outward senses are influenced by the object which is presented to them, and the intellect has an impression made on it by the outward senses.

(39) What is the meaning of the expression, "And the eyes of both of them were opened?" (Genesis 3:7). That they were not created blind is manifest even from this fact that as all other things, both animals and plants, were created in perfection, so also man must have been adorned with the things which are his most excellent parts, namely, eyes. And we may especially prove this, because a little while before the earth-born Adam was giving names to all the animals on the earth. Therefore it is perfectly plain that he saw them before doing so. Unless, indeed, Moses used the expression "eyes" in a figurative sense for the vision of the soul, by which alone the perception of good and evil, of what is elegant or unsightly, and, in fact, of all contrary natures, arise. But, if the eye is to be taken separately as counsel, which is called the warning of the understanding, then again there is a separate eye, which is a certain something devoid of sound reason, which is called opinion.

(40) What is the meaning of the expression, "Because they knew that they were naked?" (Genesis 3:7). They first arrived at the knowledge of this fact, that is to say, of their nakedness, after they had eaten of the forbidden fruit. Therefore, opinion was like the beginning of wickedness, when they perceived that they had not as yet used any covering, inasmuch as all parts of the universe are immortal and incorruptible; but they themselves immediately found themselves in need of some corruptible coverings made with hands. But this knowledge was in the nakedness itself, not as having been in itself the cause of any change, but because their mind now conceived a novelty unlike the rest of the universal world.

(41) Why they sewed fig-leaves into girdles? (Genesis 3:8). They did this in the first place, because the fruit of the fig is very pleasant and agreeable to the taste. Therefore the sacred historian here, by a symbolical expression, indicates those who sew together and join pleasures to pleasures by every means and contrivance imaginable. Therefore they bind them around the place where the parts of generation are seated, as that is the instrument of important transactions. And they do this, secondly, because although the fruit of the fig-tree is, as I have already said, sweeter than any other, yet its leaves are harder. And, therefore, Moses here wishes by this symbol to intimate that the motions of pleasure are slippery and smooth in appearance, but that they, nevertheless, are in reality hard, so that it is impossible that he who feels them should be delighted, unless he was previously sorrowful, and he will again become sorrowful. For to be always sorrowing is a melancholy thing between a double grief, the one being at its beginning, and the other coming before the first is ended.

(42) What is meant by the statement that the sound was heard of God walking in the Paradise? was it the sound of his voice, or of his feet? and can God be said to talk? (Genesis 3:8). Those gods who are in heaven, perceptible to our outward senses, walk in a ring, proceeding onwards by a circuitous track; but the Supreme Cause is steadfast and immoveable, as the ancients have decided. But the true God gives some indication also, as if he wished to give a sense of motion. For in truth even without his uttering any words, the prophets hear him, by a certain virtue of some diviner voice sounding in their ears, or perhaps being even articulately uttered. As therefore God is heard without uttering any sound, so also he gives an idea of walking when he is not walking, nay, though he is altogether immoveable. But do you not see that before they had tasted of wickedness, as they were stable and constant, and immoveable and tranquil, and uniform, so also in an equal manner must they have looked upon the Deity as immoveable, as in fact he is. But they once had become endued with cunning, they, by judging from themselves, began to strip him of his attributes of immobility and unchangeableness, and conjectured that he too was subject to variation and change.

(43) Why while they are hiding themselves from the face of God, the woman is not mentioned first, since she was the first to eat of the forbidden fruit: but why the man is spoken of in the first place; for the sacred historian's words are, "And Adam and his wife hid themselves?" (Genesis 3:9). The woman, being imperfect and depraved by nature, made the beginning of sinning and prevaricating; but the man, as being the more excellent and perfect creature, was the first to set the example of blushing and of being ashamed, and indeed, of every good feeling and action.

(44) Why they did not hide themselves in some other place, but in the middle of the trees of the Paradise? (Genesis 3:9). Every thing is not done by sinners with wisdom and sagacity, but it often happens that while thieves are watching for an opportunity of plunder, having no thoughts of the Deity who presides over the world, the booty which is close to them and lying at their feet is by some admirable management wrested from them without delay: and something of this kind took place on the present occasion. For when they ought rather to have fled to a distance from the garden in which their offence had taken place, they still were arrested in the middle of the Paradise itself, in order that they might be convicted of their sin too clearly to find any refuge even in flight itself. And this statement indicates in a figurative manner that every wicked man takes refuge in wickedness, and that every man who is wholly devoted to his passions flies to those passions as to an asylum.

(45) Why God asks Adam, "Where art thou?" when he knows everything: and why he does not also put the same question to the woman? (Genesis 3:10). The expression, "Where art thou?" does not here seem to be a mere interrogatory, but rather a threat and a conviction: "Where art thou now, O man? from how many good things art thou changed? having forsaken immortality and a life of the most perfect happiness, you have become changed to death and misery in which you are buried." But God did not condescend to put any question to the woman at all, looking upon her as the cause of the evil which had occurred, and as the guide to her husband to a life of shame. But there is an allegorical meaning in this passage, because the principal part is the man, his guide, the mind, having in itself the masculine principle, when it gives ear to any one introduces also the defect of the female part, namely that of the outward sense.

(46) Why the man says, "The woman gave me of the tree, and I did eat;" but the woman does not say, "The serpent gave to me," but, "The serpent beguiled me and I did eat?" (Genesis 3:12 - 13). The literal expression here affords grounds for that probable opinion that woman is accustomed rather to be deceived than to devise anything of importance out of her own head; but with the man the case is just the contrary. But as regards the intellect, everything which is the object of the outward senses beguiles and seduces each particular sense of every imperfect being to which it is adapted. And the sense then, being vitiated by the object, infects the dominant and principal part, the mind, with its own taint. Therefore the mind receives the impression from the outward sense, giving it that which it has received itself. For the outward sense is deceived and beguiled by the sensible object submitted to it, but the senses of the wise man are infallible, as are also the cogitations of his mind.

(47) Why God curses the serpent first, then the woman, and the man last of all? (Genesis 3:14). The reason is that the order of the verses followed the order in which the offences were committed. The first offence was the deceit practised by the serpent; the second was the sin of the woman which was owing to him when she abandoned herself to his seduction; the third thing was the guilt of the man in yielding rather to the inclination of the woman than to the commandment of God. But this order is very admirable, containing within itself a perfect allegory; inasmuch as the serpent is the emblem of desire, as is proved, and the woman of the outward sense; but the man is the symbol of intellect. Therefore the infamous author of the sin is desire; and that first deceives the outward sense, and then the outward sense captivates the mind.

(48) Why the curse is pronounced on the serpent in this manner, that he shall go on his breast and on his belly, and eat dust, and be at enmity with the woman? (Genesis 3:16). The words in themselves are plain enough, and we have evidence of them in what we have seen. But the real meaning contains an allegory concealed beneath it; since the serpent is the emblem of desire, representing under a figure a man devoted to pleasure. For he creeps upon his breast and upon his belly, being filled with meat and drink like cormorants, being inflamed by an insatiable cupidity, and being incontinent in their voracity and devouring of flesh, so that whatever relates to food is in every article something earthly, on which account he is said to eat the dust. But desire has naturally a quarrel with the outward sense, which Moses here symbolically calls the woman; but where the passions appear to be as it were guardians and champions in behalf of the senses, nevertheless they are beyond all question still more clearly flatterers forming devices against them like so many enemies; and it is the custom of those who are contending with one another to perpetrate greater evils by means of those things which they concede. Forsooth they turn the eyes to the ruin of the sight, the ears to hearing what is unwelcome; and the rest of the outward senses to insensibility. Moreover they cause dissolution and paralysis to the entire body, taking away from it all soundness, and foolishly building up instead a great number of most mischievous diseases.

(49) Why the curse pronounced against the woman is the multiplication of her sadness and groans, that she shall bring forth children in sorrow, and that her desire shall be to her husband, and that she shall be ruled over by him? (Genesis 3:16). Every woman who is the companion for life of a husband suffers all those things, not indeed as a curse but as necessary evils. But speaking figuratively, the human sense is wholly subjected to severe labour and pain, being stricken and wounded by domestic agitations. Now the following are the children in the service of the outward senses: the sight is the servant of the eyes, hearing of the ears, smelling of the nostrils, taste of the mouth, feeling of the touch. Since the life of the worthless and wicked man is full of pain and want, it arises of necessity from these facts that every thing which is done in accordance with the outward sense must be mingled with pain and fear. In respect of the mind a conversion of the outward sense takes place towards the man not as to a companion, for it, like the woman, is subject to authority as being depraved, but as to a master, because it has chosen violence rather than justice.

(50) Why God, as he had pronounced a curse on the serpent and on the woman which bore a relation to themselves and to one another, he did not pronounce a similar one upon the man, but connected the earth with him, saying, "Cursed is the earth for thy sake; in sorrow shalt thou eat of it, thorns and thistles shall it bring forth unto thee, and thou shalt eat the grass of the field: in the sweat of thy brow shalt thou eat they bread?" (Genesis 3:17). Since all intellect is a divine inspiration, God did not judge it right to curse him in the manner deserved by his offence; but converted his curse so as to fall upon the earth and his cultivation of it. But man, as a body of co-equal nature and similar character to that of the earth and understanding, is its cultivator. When the cultivator is endowed with virtue and diligence, then the body produces its proper fruit, namely sanity, an excellent state of the outward senses, strength, and beauty. But if the cultivator be a savage, then every thing is different. For the body becomes liable to a curse, since it has for its husbandman an intellect unchastised and unsound. And its fruit is nothing useful, but only thorns and thistles, sorrow and fear, and other vices which every thought strikes down, and as it were pierces the intellect with its darts. But grass here is symbolically used for food; since man has changed himself from a rational animal into a brute beast, having neglected all divine food, which is given by philosophy, by means of distinct words and laws to regulate the will.

(51) What is the meaning of the expression, "Until thou returnest to the earth from which thou wast taken;" for man was not created out of the earth alone, but also of the divine Spirit? (Genesis 3:18). In the first place it is clear, that the first man who was formed out of the earth was made up both of earth and heaven; but because he did not continue uncorrupt, but despised the commandment of God, fleeing from the most excellent part, namely, from heaven, he gave himself up wholly as a slave to the earth, the denser and heavier element. In the second place, if any one burns with a desire of virtue, which makes the soul immortal, he, beyond all question, attains to a heavenly inheritance; but because he was covetous of pleasure, by which spiritual death is engendered, he again gives himself over a second time to the earth, on which account it is said to him, "Dust thou art, and unto dust shalt thou return;" therefore the earth, as it is the beginning of a wicked and depraved man, so also it is his end; but heaven is the beginning and end of him who is endowed with virtue.

(52) Why Adam called his wife Life, and affirmed to her, "Thou art the mother of all living?" (Genesis 3:20). In the first place, Adam gave to the first created woman that familiar name of Life, inasmuch as she was destined to be the fountain of all the generations which should ever arise upon the earth after their time. In the second place, he called her by this name because she did not derive the existence of her substance out of the earth, but out of a living creature, namely, out of one part of the man, that is to say, out of his rib, which was formed into a woman, and on that account she was called "life," because she was first made out of a living creature, and because the first beings who were endowed with reason were to be generated from her. Nevertheless, it is possible that this may have been a metaphorical expression; for is not the outward sense, which is a figurative emblem of the woman, called with peculiar propriety "life?" because it is by the possession of these senses that the living being is above all other means distinguished from that which is not alive, as it is by that that the imaginations and impulses of the soul are set in motion, for the senses are the causes of each; and, in real truth the outward sense is the mother of all living creatures, for as there could be no generation without a mother, so also there could be no living creature without sense.

(53) Why God made garments of skins for Adam and his wife, and clothed them? (Genesis 3:21). Perhaps some one may laugh at the expressions here used, considering the small value of the garments thus made, as if they were not at all worthy of the labour of a Creator of such dignity and greatness; but a man who has a proper appreciation of wisdom and virtue will rightly and deservedly look upon this work as one very suitable for a God, that, namely, of teaching wisdom to those who were before labouring to no purpose; and who, having but little anxiety about procuring useful things, being seized with an insane desire for miserable honours, have given themselves up as slaves to convenience, looking upon the study of wisdom and virtue with detestation, and being in love with splendour of life and skill in mean and handicraft arts, which is in no way connected with a virtuous man. And these unhappy men do not know that a frugality, which is in need of nothing, becomes, as it were, a relation and neighbour to man, but that luxurious splendour is banished to a distance as an enemy; therefore the garment made of skins, if one should come to a correct judgment, deserves to be looked upon as a more noble possession than a purple robe embroidered with various colours. Therefore this is the literal meaning of the text; but if we look to the real meaning, then the garment of skins is a figurative expression for the natural skin, that is to say, our body; for God, when first of all he made the intellect, called it Adam; after that he created the outward sense, to which he gave the name of Life. In the third place, he of necessity also made a body, calling that by a figurative expression, a garment of skins; for it was fitting that the intellect and the outward sense should be clothed in a body as in a garment of skins; that the creature itself might first of all appear worthy of divine virtue; since by what power can the formation of the human body be put together more excellently, and in a more becoming manner, than by God? on which account he did put it together, and at the same time he clothed it; when some prepare articles of human clothing and others put them on; but this natural clothing, contemporary with the man himself, namely, the body, belonged to the same Being both to make and to clothe the man in after it was made.

(54) Who those beings are to whom God says, "Behold, Adam has become as one of us, to know good and evil?" (Genesis 3:22). The expression, "one of us," indicates a plurality of beings; unless indeed we are to suppose, that God is conversing with his own virtues, which he employed as instruments, as it were, to create the universe and all that is in it; but that expression "as," resembles an enigma, and a similitude, and a comparison, but is not declaratory of any dissimilarity; for that which is intelligible and sensibly good, and likewise that which is of a contrary character, is known to God in a different manner from that in which it is known to man; since, in the same way in which the natures of those who inquire and those who comprehend, and the things themselves too which are inquired into, and perceived, and comprehended, are distinguished, virtue itself is also capable of comprehending them. But all these things are similitudes, and forms, and images, among men; but among the gods they are prototypes, models, indications, and more manifest examples of things which are somewhat obscure; but the unborn and uncreated Father joins himself to no one, except with the intention of extending the honour of his virtues.

(55) What is the meaning of the words, "Lest perchance he put forth his hand and take of the tree of life, and eat and live for ever;" for there is no uncertainty and no envy in God? (Genesis 3:23). It is quite true that God never feels either uncertainty or envy; nevertheless he often employs ambiguous things and expressions, assenting to them as a man might do; for, as I have said before, the supreme providence is of a twofold nature, sometimes being God, and not acting in any respect as a man; but, on some occasions, as a man instructs his son, so likewise should the Lord God give warning to you. Therefore the first of these circumstances belongs to his sovereign power, and the second to his disciplinary, and to the first introduction to instruction, so as to insinuate into man's heart a voluntary inclination, since that expression, "lest perchance," is not to be taken as a proof of any hesitation on the part of God, but in relation to man, who, by his nature, is prone to hesitation, and is a denunciation of the inclinations which exist in him. For when any appearance of anything whatever occurs to any man, immediately there arises within him an impulse towards that which appears, being caused by that very thing which appears. And from this arises the second hesitating kind of uncertainty, distracting the mind in various directions, as to whether the thing is fit to be accepted, or acquired, or not. And very likely present circumstances have a respect to that second feeling; for, in truth, the Divinity is incapable of any cunning, or malevolence, or wickedness: it is absolutely impossible that God should either envy the immortality or any other good fortune belonging to any being. And we can bring the most undeniable proof of this; for it was not in consequence of any one's entreaties that he created the world; but, being a merciful benefactor, rendering an essence previously untamed and unregulated, and liable to suffering, gentle and pleasant, he did so by a vast harmony of blessings, and a regulated arrangement of them, like a chorus; and he being himself the only sure being, planted the tree of life by his own luminous character. Moreover, he was not influenced by the mediation or exhortation of any other being in communicating incorruptibility to man. But while man existed as the purest intellect, displaying no appearance either of work or of any evil discourse, he was certain to have a fitting guide, to lead him in the paths of piety, which is undoubted and genuine immortality. But from the time when he began to be converted to depravity, wishing for the things which belong to mortal life, he wandered from immortality; for it is not fitting that craft and wickedness should be rendered immortal, and moreover it would be useless to the subject; since the longer the life is which is granted to the wicked and depraved man, the more miserable is he than others, so that his immortality becomes a grave misfortune to him.

(56) Why now he calls the Paradise "pleasure," when he is sending man forth out of it to till the ground from which he was taken. (Genesis 3:23). The distinction of agriculture is conspicuous, when man in the state of paradise, practising the cultivation of wisdom as if he were employed in the cultivation of trees, and enjoying the food of imperishable and most useful fruits, was himself endowed with immortality likewise. After that, being expelled from the place of wisdom, he experienced the opposite effects of ignorance, by which the body is polluted, and at the same time the intellect is blinded, and, being exposed to a want of proper food, he wastes away, and yields to a miserable death. On which account, now, in contempt of the foolish man, God calls the Paradise "pleasure," in order to put it in opposition to a life of pain, and misery, and savageness. In truth, the life which is passed in wisdom is a pleasure, full of liberal joy, and is the constant enjoyment of a rational soul; but that life which is destitute of wisdom is found to be both savage and miserable, although it is excessively deceived by the appetites, which pain both precedes and follows.

(57) Why God places a cherubim in front of the Paradise, and a flaming sword, which turned every way, to keep the way of the tree of life? (Genesis 3:24). The name cherubim designates the two original virtues which belong to the Deity, namely, his creative and his royal virtues. The one of which has the title of God, the other, or the royal virtue, that of Lord. Now the form of the creative power is a peaceable, and gentle, and beneficent virtue; but the royal power is a legislative, and chastising, and correcting virtue. Moreover, by the flaming sword he here symbolically intimates the heaven: for the air is of a flaming colour, and turns itself round, revolving about the universe. Therefore, all these things assumed to themselves the guardianship of the Paradise, because they are the presidents over wisdom, like a mirror; since, to illustrate my meaning by an example, the wisdom of the world is a sort of mirror of the divine virtues, in the similitude of which it was perfected, and by which the universe and all the things in it are regulated and arranged. But the way to wisdom is called philosophy (a word which means the love or the pursuit of wisdom). And since the creative virtue is endued with philosophy, being both philosophical and royal, so also the world itself is philosophical. Some persons however have fancied that it is the sun which is indicated by the flaming sword; because, by its constant revolutions and turnings every way, it marks out the seasons of the year, as being the guardian of human life and of every thing which serves to the life of all men.

(58) Whether it was properly said with respect to Cain: "I have gotten a man from the Lord?" (Genesis 4:1). Here there is a distinction made, as to-from some one, and out of some one, and by some thing. Out of some one, as out of materials; from some one, as from a cause; and by some thing, as by an instrument. But the Father and Creator of all the world is not an instrument, but a cause. Therefore he wanders from right wisdom who says, "That what has been made has been made, not from God, but by God."

(59) Why the sacred historian first describes the employment of the younger brother, Abel, saying: "He was a keeper of sheep; but Cain was a cultivator of the earth?" (Genesis 4:2). Since, although the virtuous son was in point of time younger than the wicked son, yet in point of virtue he was older. On which account, on the present occasion, when their actions are to be compared together, he is placed first. Therefore one of them exercises a business, and takes care of living creatures, although they are devoid of reason, gladly taking upon himself the employment of a shepherd, which is a princely office, and as it were a sort of rehearsal of royal power; but the other devotes his attention to earthly and inanimate objects.

(60) Why Cain after some days offers up the first-fruits of his fruits, but when it is said that "Abel offered up first-fruits of the first-born of his flock and of the fat," "after some days" is not added? (Genesis 4:3 - 4). Moses here intimates the difference between a lover of himself, and one who is thoroughly devoted to God; for the one took to himself the first-fruits of his fruits, and very impiously looked upon God as worthy only of the secondary and inferior offerings; for the expression, "after some days," implies that he did not do so immediately; and when it is said that he offered of the fruits, that intimates that he did not offer of the best fruits which he had, and herein displays his iniquity. But the other, without any delay, offered up the first-born and eldest of all his flocks, in order that in this the Father might not be treated unworthily.

(61) Why, when he had begun with Cain, he still mentions him here in the second place, when he says: "And God had respect unto Abel and unto his offerings; but unto Cain and unto his sacrifices he paid no attention?" (Genesis 4:5). In the first place, because the good man, who is by nature first, is not at first perceived by the outward senses of any man except in his own turn, and by people of virtuous conduct. Secondly, because the good and the wicked man are two distinct characters; he accepts the good man, seeing that he is a lover of what is good, and an eager student of virtue; but he rejects and regards with aversion the wicked man, presuming that he will be prone to that side by the order of nature. Therefore he says here with exceeding fitness, that God had regard, not to the offerings, but to those who offered them, rather than to the gifts themselves; for men have regard to and regulate their approbation by the abundance and richness of offerings, but God looks at the sincerity of the soul, having no regard to ambition or illusion of any kind.

(62) What is the meaning of the distinction here made between a gift and a sacrifice? (Genesis 4:4). The man who slays a sacrifice, after having made a division, pours the blood around the altar and takes the flesh home; but he who offers it as a gift, offers as it should seem the whole to him who accepts it. Therefore, the man who is a lover of self is a distributor, like Cain; but he who is a lover of God is the giver of a free gift, as was Abel.

(63) How it was that Cain became aware that his offering had not pleased God? (Genesis 4:5). Perhaps he resolved his doubts, an additional cause being added, for sorrow seized upon him and his countenance fell. Therefore, he took the sorrow which he felt as an indication that he had been sacrificing what was not pleasing or approved of, when joy and happiness would have been suited to one who was sacrificing with purity of heart and spirit.

(64) Why is it that the expression used is not, because you do not offer rightly; but, because (or unless) you do not divide rightly? (Genesis 4:7). In the first place, we must understand that right division and improper division are nothing else but order and the want of it. And it is by order that the universal world and its parts were made; since the Creator of the world, when he began to arrange and regulate the previously untamed and unarranged power which was liable to suffering, employed section and division. For he placed the heavy elements which were prone to descend downwards by their own nature, namely, the earth and the water, in the centre of the universe; but he placed the air and the fire at a greater altitude, as they were raised on high by reason of their lightness. But separating and dividing the pure nature, namely heaven, he carried it round and diffused it over the universe, so that it should be completely invisible to all men; containing within itself the whole universe in all its parts. Again, the statement that animals and plants are produced out of seeds, some moist and some dry, what else does it mean but the inevitable dissection and separation of distinction? Therefore it follows inevitably, that this order and arrangement of the universe must be imitated in all things, especially in feeling and acknowledging gratitude; by which we are invited to requite in some degree and manner the kindnesses of those who have showered greater benefits liberally on us. Moreover, to pay one's thanks to God is an action which is intrinsically right in itself: and it is not to be disapproved of that he should receive the offerings due to him at the earliest moment, and fresh gifts from the first-fruits of every thing, not being dishonoured by any negligence on our part. Since it is not fitting that man should reserve for himself the first and most excellent things which are created, and should offer what is only second best to the all-wise God and Creator; for that division would be faulty and blameworthy, showing a most preposterous and unnatural arrangement.

(65) What is the meaning of the expression: "You have done wrongly; now rest?" (Genesis 4:8). He is here giving very useful advice; since, to do no wrong at all is the greatest of all good things: but he who sins, and who thus blushes and is overwhelmed with shame, is near akin to him, being, if I may use such a phrase, as the younger brother to the elder; for those persons who pride themselves on their errors as if they had not done wrong, are afflicted with a disease which is difficult to cure, or rather which is altogether incurable.

(66) Why he seems to be giving what is good into the hand of a wicked man, when he says, "And unto thee shall be his desire?" (Genesis 4:8). He does not deliver good into his hand; but the expression is heard with different feelings; since he is speaking, not of a pious man, but after the action is accomplished, saying of him: The desire and respect of the impiety of this man's wickedness will be towards you. Do not therefore talk about necessity, but about your own habits, in order that thus he may represent the voluntary action. And again, the sentence, "And you shall be his ruler over him," has a reference to the operation. In the first place, you begin to act with wickedness; and now behold, another iniquity follows that great and injurious iniquity. Therefore, he both thinks and affirms that this is the principal part of all voluntary injury.

(67) Why he slew his brother in the field? (Genesis 4:9). That as all in fecundity and sterility arises from a neglect of sowing and planting land a second time, he may be kept continually in mind of his wicked murder, and self-blamed for it; since the ground was not to be the same for the future, after it was compelled, contrary to its nature, to drink of human blood, to bring forth food to that man who imbued it with the polluted stain of blood.
(68) Why he who knows all things asks the fratricide: "Where is thy brother Abel?" (#Ge 4:10). He puts this question to him because he wishes the man to confess voluntarily and spontaneously, of his own accord, so that he may not imagine that every thing is done out of necessity; for he who had slain another through necessity, would have confessed unwillingly, as having done the deed unwillingly; since that which does not depend upon ourselves does not deserve accusation; but the man who has done wrong intentionally denies it; for those who do wrong are liable to repentance. Therefore, he has interwoven this principle in all parts of his legislation, because the Deity himself is never the cause of evil.
(69) Why he who had slain his brother makes answer as if he were replying to a man; and says, "I do not know: am I my brother's keeper?" (Genesis 4:9). It is the opinion of an atheist to think that the eye of God does not penetrate through every thing, and behold all things at the same time; piercing not only through what is visible, but also through every thing which lurks in the deepest and bottomless unfathomable abysses. Suppose a person said to him, "How can you be ignorant where your brother is, and how is it that you do not know that, when as yet he is one out of the only four human beings which exist in the world? He being one with both his parents, and you his only brother." To this question the reply made is: "I am not my brother's keeper." O what a beautiful apology! And whose keeper and protector ought you to have been, rather than your brother's? But if you have excited your diligence to give effect to violence, and injury, and fraud, and homicide, which are the foulest and most abominable of actions, why did you consider the safety of your brother a secondary object?"
(70) What is the meaning of the expression, "The voice of thy brother's blood cries to me out of the earth?" (Genesis 4:10). This is especially an example by which to take warning; for the Deity listens to those who are worthy, although they be dead, knowing that they are alive as to an incorporeal life. But he averts his countenance from the prayers of the wicked, although they are living a flourishing life, inasmuch as he looks upon them as dead to any real life, carrying about their bodies like a sepulchre; and having buried their miserable souls in it.
(71) Why he is said to be cursed upon the earth? (Genesis 4:11). The earth is the last portion of the world, therefore if that utters curses, we must consider that the other elements do likewise pour forth adequate maledictions; for instance, the fountains, and rivers, and sea, and the air, and the land, and the fire, and

the light, and the sun, and moon, and stars, and in short the whole heaven. For if inanimate and earthly nature, throwing off the yoke, wars against injury, why may not still rather those natures do so which are of a purer character? But as for him, against whom the parts of the world carry on war, what hope of safety he can have for the future, I know not.

(72) What is the meaning of the curse, "You shall be groaning and trembling upon the earth?" (Genesis 4:13).{6}{our translation is, "My punishment is greater than I can bear."} This also is a general principle; for in all evils there are some things which are perceived immediately, and some which are felt at a later period; for those which are future cause fear, and those which are felt at once bring sorrow.

(73) What is the meaning of Cain saying, "My punishment is too great for you to dismiss me? (Genesis 4:12). In truth there is not misery greater than to be deserted and despised by God; for the anarchy of fools is cruel and very intolerable; but to be despised by the great King, and to fall down as an abject person cast down from the government of the Supreme Power is an indescribable affliction.

(74) What is the meaning of Cain, when he says, "Everyone who shall find me will kill me:" when there was scarcely another human being in the world except his parents? (Genesis 4:14). In the first place he might have received injury from the parts of the world which indeed were made for the advantage of the good and that they might partake of them, but which nevertheless, derived from the wicked no slight degree of revenge. In the second place it may be that he said this, because he was apprehensive of injury from beasts, and reptiles; for nature has brought forth these animals with the express object of their being instruments of vengeance on the wicked. In the third place, some people may imagine that he is speaking with reference to his parents, on whom he had inflicted an unprecedented sorrow, and the first evil which had happened to them, before they knew what death was.

(75) Why whoever should slay Cain should be liable to bear a sevenfold punishment? (Genesis 4:15). As our soul consists of eight portions, being accustomed to be divided in its rational and irrational individuality into seven subordinate parts, namely into the five outward senses, and the instrument of vice, and the faculty of generation; those seven parts exist among the causes of wickedness and evil, on which account they likewise fall under judgment; but the death of the principal and dominant portion of man, namely of the mind, is principally the wickedness which exists in it. Whoever therefore slays the mind, mingling in it folly, and insensibility, instead of sense, will cause dissolution also of the seven irrational parts; since, just as the principal and leading part had a portion from virtue, in the same manner likewise are its subject divisions composed.

(76) Why a sign is put on him who had slain his brother, that no one should kill him who found him; when it would have been natural to do the contrary, namely, to give him over to the hands of an executioner to be put to death? (Genesis 4:16). This is said because, in the first place, the change of the nature of living is one kind of death; but continual sorrow and unmixed fear are destitute of joy and devoid of all good hope, and so they bring on many terrible and various evils which are so many sensible deaths. In the second place, the sacred historian designs at the very beginning of his work to enunciate the law about the incorruptibility of the soul, and to confute as deceitful those who look upon the life which is contained in this body as the only happy life; for behold one of the two brothers is guilty of those enormous crimes which have already been mentioned, namely, impiety and fratricide; and he is still alive, and begetting offspring, and building cities. But the other who was praised in respect of his piety is treacherously put to death; while the voice of the Lord not only clearly cries out that that existence which is perceptible by the outward senses is not good, and that such a death is not evil, but also that that life which is in the flesh is not life, but that there is another give to man free from old age, and more immortal, which the incorporeal souls have received; for that expression of the poet about Scylla, is asserted in the same familiarity about a person who lives ill and passes a long life for many years in the practice of wickedness. In the third place, since Cain had perpetrated this fratricide of enormous guilt above all other crimes, he presents himself to him, quite forgetful of the injury that he has done, imposing on all judges a most peaceful law for the first crime; not that they are not to destroy malefactors, but that resting for a while with great patience and long suffering, they shall study compassion rather than severity. But God himself, with the most perfect wisdom, has laid down the rule of familiarity and intelligence with reference to the first sinner: not slaying the homicide, but destroying him in another manner; since he scarcely permitted him to be enumerated among the generations of his father, but shows him proscribed not only by his parents but by the whole race of mankind, allotting him a state separate from that of others, and secluded from the class of rational animals, as one who had been expelled, and banished, and turned into the nature of beasts.

(77) Why Lamech, after the fifth generation, blames himself for the fratricide of his elder Cain; saying, as the scripture reports, to his wives, Adah and Zillah; "I have slain a man to my injury and a young man to my hurt; since if vengeance is taken upon Cain sevenfold, it shall certainly be taken on Lamech seventy and sevenfold?" (Genesis 4:23). In numerals one is before ten, both in order and in virtue, for it is the first beginning and element and measure of all things. But the number ten is subsequent, and is measured by the other, being inferior to it, both in order and virtue; therefore, also, the number seven is antecedent in its origin to and more ancient than the number seventy, but the number seventy is younger than the number seven, and contains the calculation of generations. These premises being laid down, he who first committed sin, as if he had been really always ignorant of evil, like the first odd number, namely, the unit, is chastised more simply; but the second offender, because he had the first for an example, so that there cannot possibly be any excuse made for him, is guilty of a voluntary crime, and because he did not receive honourable wisdom from that more simple punishment, the consequence will be that he will both suffer all that first punishment, and will, moreover, receive this second one, which is contained in the number ten. For as in the horse-races they pay the groom who has trained the horse twice as great a reward as they give to the driver, so some wicked men, inclined to acts of injustice, gain the miserable triumph of victory and then are punished with a double punishment, both by the first one which is contained in the unit, and also by the second which is contained in the number ten; besides, Cain being the author of a homicide, when he was ignorant of the greatness of the pollution which he was incurring, because no death had hitherto taken place in the world, suffered a more simple punishment, namely, only a sevenfold penalty in the order of the unit; but as his imitator could not take refuge in the same plea of ignorance, he ought to be subjected to a twofold punishment, not only to one equal and similar to that which had been inflicted on the first offender, but also another, which should be the seventh among the decades. In truth, according to the law, the trial which is before the tribunal is a sevenfold one; first of all, the eyes are put on their trial, because they beheld what was not lawful; secondly, the ears are impeached, because they heard what they ought not to have heard; thirdly, the smell is brought into question, as having been reduced by smoke and vapour; fourthly, the taste is accused, as being subservient to the pleasures of the belly; fifthly, a charge is brought against the taste, by means of which, besides the operations of the senses abovementioned, in respect of those things which prevail over the spirit, other things, also, are superadded separately, such as the takings of cities, the captivities of men, the destructions of those citadels of cities in which wisdom dwells; sixthly, an accusation is urged against the tongue and other instruments of speech, for being silent as to what should be spoken of, and speaking of what should be buried in silence; and, in the seventh place, the lower part of the belly is impeached for inflaming and exciting the passions by immoderate lust. This is the meaning of that expression, according to which a sevenfold vengeance was taken upon Cain, but a seventy and sevenfold vengeance upon Lamech for the causes above mentioned, because he was the second offender, not having been taught by the punishment of the first delinquent, and therefore he is altogether worthy to receive his punishment, which is the more simple one, like the unit in numerals, and, also, a manifold punishment too equal to the number ten.

(78) Why Adam, when he begat Seth, introduces him saying, "God has raised up for me another seed in the place of Abel whom Cain slew?" (Genesis 4:25). In real truth Seth is another seed and the beginning of a second nativity of Abel, in accordance with a certain natural principle; for Abel is like to one who comes down below from above, on which account it was that he perished injuriously; but Seth resembles one who is proceeding upwards from below, on which account he also increases. And in proof of this argument Abel is explained as having been brought back and offered upwards to God. But it is not proper that everything should be raised and borne upwards, but only that which is good, for God is in no respect whatever the cause of evil. Therefore, whatever is indistinct and uncertain, and mingled, and in confusion and disorder, has also, very properly, blame and praise mingled together: praise, because it honours the cause, and blame, since as the occurrence happened fortuitously, so it is without any plans having been formed or any gratitude expressed. Moreover, nature also separated the two sons from him; it rendered the good one worthy of immortality, resolving him into a voice interceding with God; but the wicked one it gave over to corruption. But the name Seth is interpreted "watered," according to the variation of plants which grow by being watered, and put forth shoots and bear fruit. But these things are the symbols of the soul, so that it is not lawful to assert that the Divinity is the cause of all things equally, of the bad as well as of the good, but only of the good, and that alone ought to be planted alive.

(79) Why Enos, the son of Seth, hoped to call upon the name of the Lord God? (Genesis 4:26). The name Enos is interpreted "man;" and it is received as meaning, not the whole of the combined man, but as the rational part of the soul, namely, the intellect, to which it is peculiarly becoming to hope, for irrational animals are devoid of hope; but hope is a sort of presage of joy, and before joy there is an expectation of good things.

(80) Why, after the mention of hope, Moses says, "This is the book of the generations of men?" (Genesis 5:1). It is by this that he made what has been said before worthy of belief. What is man? Man is a being which, beyond all other races of animals, has received a copious and wonderful portion of hope; and this is as it were inscribed on his very nature, and celebrated there; for the human intellect hopes by its own nature.

(81) Why, in the genealogy of Adam, Moses no longer mentions Cain, but only Seth, who, he says, was according to his appearance and form; on which account he proceeds to retain the generations which descend from him in his genealogy? (Genesis 5:3). It can neither be lawful to enumerate a wicked and sinful murderer either in the list of reason or in that of number; for he must be cast out like dung, as some one said, looking upon him as one of such a character; and on this account the sacred historian neither points him out as the successor of his father who had been formed out of the dust, nor as the head of succeeding generations; but he distributes both these characteristics to him who was without pollution, and names Seth, who is a drinker of water, as having been watered by his father, and as begetting hope in his own increase and progress; on which account it is not inconsiderately and foolishly that he says that he was born according to the form and appearance of his father, to the reproof of his elder brother, who, on account of the foulness of the murder which he had committed, has nothing in him resembling his father, either in body or soul. And on this account Moses has separated him from the family, and has given his share to his brother, being the noble privilege of the birthright of the first-born.

(82) What is the meaning of the verse, Enoch pleased God after he begat Methuselah, two hundred years? (Genesis 5:22). God appointed by the law the fountains of all good things to be under the principles of generation itself. And what I mean is something of this sort. A little while before he appointed mercy and pardon to exist, now again he decrees that penitence shall exist, not in any degree mocking or reproaching these men, who are believed to have offended, and at the same time giving the soul an opportunity to mount up from wickedness to virtue, like the conversion of those who are proceeding towards a snare. For behold, the man being made a husband and a father together with his birth, makes a beginning of honesty. And he is said to please God, for although he does not persevere in piety from the moment that he is born, nevertheless, all that remaining period is counted to him as having been spent in a praiseworthy mode of life, because he pleased God for so many years. And these things are said, not because it perhaps was, but it might perhaps have seemed different; but he approves of the order of things, for indulgence having been exemplified, in this case of Cain, after no long interval of time, he introduces this statement, that Enoch practised repentance, warning us by it that repentance alone can procure indulgence.

(83) Why Enoch, who cultivated repentance, is said to have lived before his repentance a hundred and sixty-five years, but two hundred after his repentance? (Genesis 5:22).{8}{this is at variance with the statement in the Bible, which says he lived sixty-five years before the birth of Methuselah, and walked with God three hundred years.} This number of a hundred and sixty-five is combined of the singular addition of ten numbers from the unit to ten; as one, two, three, four, five, six, seven, eight, nine, ten, the total of which is fifty five. And again, from that by the addition of ten numbers, which, removing the unit proceed upwards by twos, and two, four, six, eight, ten, twelve, fourteen, sixteen, eighteen, twenty, which make a hundred and ten; the combination of which, with the numbers first mentioned, produces a hundred and sixty-five; and in this addition the even numbers amount to twice as much as the odd numbers; for the woman is more violent than the man, in the preposterous manner in which the wicked man rules over the virtuous man, the outward sense over the mind, the body over the outward sense, and matter over its cause. But the number two hundred, in which repentance was practised, is combined of two numbers of one hundred, the first hundred of which intimates a purification from injustice, but the other indicates the plenitude of perfect virtue. In truth, before anything else is done, the first thing is to cut off from a sick body every diseased part, and after that means of cure are to be applied to it, for this is the first step, and the other the second. Moreover, the number two hundred consists of fours, for it is produced as from seed, from four triangular numbers, and from four tetragons, and from four pentagons, and from four hexagons, and from four heptagons; and, as one may say, it fixes its step on the number seven. Now the four triangles are these, one, three, six, ten, which make twenty; the four tetragons are one, four, nine, sixteen, which make thirty; from the four pentagons, one, five, twelve, twenty-two, is made the number forty. Moreover, the four hexagons, one, six, fifteen, twenty-eight, make fifty; and the four heptagons, one, seven, eighteen, thirty-four, make sixty; and all these numbers put together make two hundred.

(84) Why the man who lives a life of repentance is said to have lived three hundred and sixty-five years? (Genesis 5:23). In the first place, the year contains three hundred and sixty-five days; therefore, by the symbol of the solar orbit, the sacred historian here indicates the life of the repentant man. In the second place, as the sun is the cause of day and night, performing his revolutions by day above the hemisphere of the earth, and his course by night under the earth, so also the life of the man of repentance consists of alternations of light and darkness; of darkness, that is, of times of agitation and circumstances of injury; and of light, when the light of virtue and its radiant brilliancy arises. In the third place, he has assigned to him a complete number, as the sun is ordained to be the chief of the stars of heaven, under an appointed number, in the time which came before the period of his repentance, to lead to the oblivion of the sins previously committed; since, as God is good, he bestows the greatest favours most abundantly, and, at the same time, he effaces the former offences of those who devote themselves to him, and which might deserve chastisement, by a recollection of their virtues.

(85) Why, when Enoch died, the sacred historian adds the assertion, "He pleased God?" (Genesis 5:24). In the first place, he says this because, by such a statement, he implies that the soul is immortal, inasmuch as after it is stripped of the body, it still pleases a second time. In the second place, he honours the repentant man with praise, because he has persevered in the same alteration of manners, and has never receded till he has arrived at complete perfection of life; for behold, some men appear to be readily sated after they have only tasted of excellence; and after a hope of recovery has been given to them, they relapse again into the same disease.

(86) What is the meaning of the expression, "He was not found because God translated him?" (Genesis 5:24). In the first place, the end of virtuous and holy men is not death but a translation and migration, and an approach to some other place of abode. In the second place, in this instance something marvellous did take place; for he was supposed to be carried off in such a way as to be invisible, for then he was not found: and a proof of this is, that he was sought for as being invisible, not only as having been carried away from their sight, since translation into another place is nothing else than a placing of a person in another situation; but it is here suggested, that he was translated from a visible place, perceptible by the outward senses, into an incorporeal idea, appreciable only to the intellect. This mercy also was bestowed on the great prophet, for his sepulchre also was known to no one. And besides these two there was another, Elijah, who ascended from the things of earth into heaven, according to the divine appearance which was then presented to him, and who thus followed higher things, or, to speak with more exact propriety, was raised up to heaven.

(87) How it was that immediately upon the nativity of Noah his father says, "He will make us rest from labours and sorrows, and from the earth, which the Lord God has cursed?" (Genesis 5:29). The fathers of the saints did not prophesy except for grave reasons and on important occasions; for although those who were rendered worthy of prophetical panegyric did not prophecy at all times or on all subjects, they did so at all events on one occasion and on one subject, with which they were acquainted. Nor is this of no importance, but it is an emblem and an example, since Noah is a kind of surname of righteousness, of which, when the intellect is made a partaker, it causes us to rest from all wicked works, and releases us from sorrows and from fears, and renders us secure and joyful. It also causes us to rest from that earthly nature which has been previously laid under a curse, which this body, when affected by pain, is connected with, especially in those persons who give cause for it, and who wear out their lives with pleasure. Nevertheless, if we examine attentively the events and circumstances, and compare them with the letter of the scriptures, the prophecy which has been already produced is deceived, because, in the time of this man, there did not arise any putting down of evils, but a more vehement obstinacy in sin and great afflictions, and the unprecedented event of the deluge. But you must note carefully, that Noah is the tenth in generation from the earth-born Adam.

(88) What is meant by the three sons of Noah being named Shem, Ham, and Japhet? (Genesis 5:32). These names are the symbols of three human things, what is good, what is bad, and what is indifferent; Shem is the symbol of what is good, Ham of what is bad, and Japhet of what is indifferent.

(89) Why from the time that the deluge drew near, the human race is said to have increased so as to become a multitude? (Genesis 6:1). Divine mercies do always precede judgment; since the first work of God is to do good, and to destroy follows afterwards; but he himself (when terrible evils are about to happen) loves to provide and is accustomed to provide that previously an abundance of many and great blessings shall be produced. On this principle also Egypt, when there was about to be a barrenness and famine for seven years as the prophet himself says, {9}{Genesis 41:28.} was for an equal number of years continuously made exceedingly fertile by the beneficent and saving power of the Creator of the universe. And in the same way in which he showers benefits upon men, he also teaches them to depart and to abstain from sin; that these blessings may not be turned into the contrary. And on this account now, by the freedom of their institutions, the cities of the world have increased in generous virtue, so that if any corruption supervenes subsequently they may disapprove of their own acts of wickedness as extraordinary and irremediable; not at all looking upon the divinity as the cause of them, for that has no connection with wickedness or misery, for the task of the Deity is only to bestow blessings.

(90) What is the meaning of the expression, "My spirit shall not always strive with man, because he is but flesh?" (Genesis 6:3). An oracle is here promulgated as if it were a law; for the divine spirit is not a motion of the air, but intellect and wisdom; just as it also flows over the man who with great skill constructed the tabernacle of the Lord, namely upon Bezaleel, when the scripture says, "And he filled him with the divine spirit of wisdom and understanding." Therefore that spirit comes upon men, but does not abide or persevere in them; and the Lord himself adds the reason, when he says, "Because they are flesh." For the disposition of the flesh is inconsistent with wisdom, inasmuch as it makes a bond of alliance with desire; on which account it is evident that nothing important can be in the way of incorporeal and light souls, or can be any hindrance to their discerning and comprehending the condition of nature, because a pure disposition is acquired together with constancy.

(91) Why it is said that the days of man shall be a hundred and twenty years? (Genesis 6:4). God appears here to fix the limit of human life by this number, indicating by it the manifold prerogative of honour; for in the first place this number proceeds from the units, according to combination, from the number fifteen; but the principle of the number fifteen is that of a more transparent appearance, since it is on the fifteenth day that the moon is rendered full of light, borrowing its light of the sun at the approach of evening, and restoring it to him again in the morning; so that during the night of the full moon the darkness is scarcely visible, but it is all light. In the second place, the number a hundred and twenty is a triangular number, and is the fifteenth number consisting of triangles. Thirdly, it is so because it consists of a combination of odd and even numbers, being contained by the power of the faculty of the concurring numbers, sixty-four and fifty-six; for the equal number of sixty-four is compounded of the uniting of these eight odd numbers, one, three, five, seven, nine, eleven, thirteen, fifteen; the reduction of which, by their parts into squares, makes a sum total of sixty-four, and that is a cube, and at the same time a square number. But again from the seven double units there arises the unequal number of fifty-six, being compounded of seven double pairs, which generate other productions of them, two, four, six, eight, ten, twelve, fourteen; the sum total of which is fifty-six. In the fourth place, it is compounded of four numbers, of one triangle, namely fifteen; and of another square, namely twenty-five; and of a third quinquangular figure, thirty-five; and of a fourth a sexangular figure forty-five, by the same analogy: for the fifth is always received according to each appearance; for from the unity of the triangles the fifth number becomes fifteen; again the fifth of the quadrangular number from the unit makes twenty-five; and the fifth of the quinquangular number from the unit makes thirty-five; and the fifth of the sexangular number from the unit makes forty-five. But every one of these numbers is a divine and sacred number, consisting of fifteens as has been already shown; and the number twenty-five belongs to the tribe of Levi.{10}{see Numbers 8:24.} And the number thirty-five comes from the double diagram of arithmetic, geometry, and harmony; but sixteen, and eighteen, and nineteen, and twenty-one, the combination of which numbers amounts to seventy-four, is that according to which seven months' children are born. And forty-five consists of a triple diagram; but to this number, sixteen, nineteen, twenty-two, and twenty-eight, belong: the combination of which makes eighty-five, according to which nine months' children are produced. Fifthly, this diagram has fifteen parts, and a twofold composition, peculiarly belonging to itself; forsooth when divided by two it gives sixty, the measure of the age of all mankind; when divided by three it gives forty, the idea of prophecy; when divided by four it gives thirty, a nation; when divided by five, it makes twenty-four, the measure of day and night; when divided by six, it gives twenty, a beginning; when divided by eight, we have fifteen, the moon in the fulness of brilliancy; when divided by ten, it makes twelve, the zodiac embellished with living animals; when divided by twelve, it makes ten, holy; when divided by fifteen, it gives eight, the first ark; when divided by twenty, it leaves six, the number of creation; when divided by twenty-four, it makes five, the emblem of the outward sense; when divided by thirty it makes four, the beginning of solid measure; when divided by forty, it gives three, the symbol of fulness, the beginning, the middle, and the end; when divided by sixty, it makes two, which is woman; and when divided by the whole number of a hundred and twenty, the product is one, or man. And every one of all these numbers is more natural, as is proved in each of them, but the composition of them is twofold, for the product is two hundred and forty, which is a sign that it is worthy of a twofold life; for as the number of years is doubled, so also we may imagine that the life is doubled too; one being in connection with the body, the other being detached from the body, according to which every holy and perfect man may receive the gift of prophecy. Sixthly, because the fifth and sixth figures arise, the three numbers being multiplied together, three times four times five, since three times four times five make sixty; so in like manner the next following numbers four times five times six make a hundred and twenty, for four times five times six make a hundred and twenty. Seventhly, when the number twenty has been taken in, which is the beginning of the reduction of mankind, I mean twenty, and being added to itself two or three times, so as to make twenty, forty, and sixty, these added together make a hundred and twenty. But perhaps the number a hundred and twenty is not the general term of human life, but only of the life of those men who existed at that time, and who were to perish by the deluge after an interval of so many years, which their kind Benefactor prolonged, giving them space for repentance; when, after the aforesaid term, they lived a longer time in the subsequent ages.

(92) On what principle it was that giants were born of angels and women? (#Ge 6:4). The poets call those men who were born out of the earth giants, that is to say, sons of the Earth.{11}{the Greek name Gigas is said to be derived from geµ and gennaoµ, "to bring forth."} But Moses here uses this appellation improperly, and he uses it too very often merely to denote the vast personal size of the principal men, equal to that of Hajk12}{hajk is an addition of the Armenian translator; it is the name of a fabulous patriarch of the Armenian nation.} or Hercules. But he relates that these giants were sprung from a combined procreation of two natures, namely, from angels and mortal women; for the substance of angels is spiritual; but it occurs every now and then that on emergencies occurring they have imitated the appearance of men, and transformed themselves so as to assume the human shape; as they did on this occasion, when forming connexions with women for the production of giants. But if the children turn out imitators of the wickedness of their mothers, departing from the virtue of their fathers, let them depart, according to the determination of the will of a depraved race, and because of their proud contempt for the supreme Deity, and so be condemned as guilty of voluntary and deliberate wickedness. But sometimes Moses styles the angels the sons of God, inasmuch as they were not produced by any mortal, but are incorporeal, as being spirits destitute of any body; or rather that exhorter and teacher of virtue, namely Moses, calls those men who are very excellent and endowed with great virtue the sons of God; and the wicked and depraved men he calls bodies, or flesh.

(93) What is the meaning of the expression: "God considered anxiously, because he had made man upon the earth; and he resolved the matter in his mind?" (Genesis 6:6).{13}{the translation of our Bible is, "It repented God that he had made man upon the earth."} Some persons imagine that it is intimated by these words that the Deity repented; but they are very wrong to entertain such an idea, since the Deity is unchangeable. Nor are the facts of his caring and thinking about the matter, and of his agitating it in his mind, any proofs that he is repenting, but only indications of a kind and determinate counsel, according to which the displays care, revolving in his mind the cause why he had made man upon the earth. But since this earth is a place of misery, even that heavenly being, man, who is a mixture compounded of soul and body, from the very hour of his birth to that of his death, is nothing else but the slave of the body. That the Deity therefore should meditate and deliberate on these matters is nothing surprising; since most men take to themselves wickedness rather than virtue, being influenced by the twofold impulse mentioned above; namely, that of a body by its nature corruptible, and placed in the terrible situation of earth, which is the lowest of all places.

(94) Why God, after having threatened to destroy mankind, says that he will also destroy all the beasts likewise; using the expression, "from man to beast, and from creeping things to flying creatures;" for how could irrational animals have committed sin? (Genesis 6:7). This is the literal statement of the holy scripture, and it informs us that animals were not necessarily and in their primary cause created for their own sake, but for the sake of mankind and to act as the servants of men; and when the men were destroyed, it followed necessarily and naturally that they also should be destroyed with them, as soon as the men, for whose sake they had been made, had ceased to exist. But as to the hidden meaning conveyed by the statement, since man is a symbol for the intellect which exists in us, and animals for the outward sense, when the chief creature has first been depraved and corrupted by wickedness, all the outward sense also perishes with him, because he had no relics whatever of virtue, which is the cause of salvation.

(95) Why God says, I am indignant that I made them? (Genesis 6:7). In the first place, Moses is here again relating what took place, as if he were speaking of some illustrious action of man, but, properly speaking, God does not feel anger, but is exempt from, and superior to, all such perturbations of spirit. Therefore Moses wishes here to point out, by an extravagant form of expression, that the iniquities of man had grown to such a height, that they stirred up and provoked to anger even that very Being who by his nature was incapable of anger. In the second place he warns us, by a figure, that foolish actions are liable to punishment, but that those which proceed from wise and deliberate counsel are praiseworthy.

(96) Why it is afterwards said, that Noah found grace in the sight of the Lord? (Genesis 6:8). In the first place, the time calls for a comparison; since all the rest of mankind has been rejected for their ingratitude, he places the just man in the place of them all, asserting that he had found favour with God, not because he alone was deserving of favour, when the whole universal body of the human race had had benefits and mercies heaped on them, but because he alone had seemed to be mindful of the kindnesses which he had received. In the second place, when the whole generation had been given over to destruction, with the exception of one single family, it followed inevitably that that remaining household should be asserted to have shown itself worthy of the divine grace, that it might be, as it were, a seed and a spark of a new race of mankind. And what could be a greater grace and mercy than that the man, of whom this is said, should be at the same time the end and beginning of the family of mankind?

(97) Why does Moses enumerate the generations of Noah with reference not to his ancestors but to his virtues? (Genesis 6:9). He does this in the first place, because all the men of that age were wicked: secondly, he is here imposing a law upon the will, because, to an anxious follower of virtue, virtue itself stands in the place of a real generation, if indeed men are the means of the generation of men, but the virtues of minds. And on this account it is that he says, he was a just man, perfect, and one who pleased God; but justice, and perfection, and grace before God, are the greatest of virtues.

(98) What was the meaning of Moses when he says, "And all the earth was corrupt in the sight of God, and the earth was filled with iniquity?" (Genesis 6:11). Moses himself has given us the reason why he speaks thus, in the sentence in which he asserts that iniquity had arisen by reason of the corruption of the earth; for deliverance from iniquity is righteousness, both in all the parts of the world, in heaven, that is, and earth, and among men.

(99) What is the meaning of his saying, "All flesh had corrupted his way upon the earth?" (Genesis 6:12). In the first place, the sacred historian calls the man who is devoted to the love of himself, flesh; therefore, when he had already said he was flesh, he introduces not the same flesh, but the flesh of the same being, namely, of man, or perhaps he is speaking even of man abstractedly considered; for every one who passes a life destitute of all civilisation, and bewildered by intemperance, is flesh. In the second place, he supposes here the cause of spiritual corruption to be, as in truth it is, the flesh, because that is the seat of desire; and from it, as from a living spring, arise all the peculiar appetites, and passions, and other affections. In the third place, he very naturally says, that all flesh had corrupted his way; for "his" is a partial case, declined from the nominative case of the pronoun "he, she, or it;" for as for the being to whom we refer honour, we scarcely dare to speak of him by his own name, but we call him He. And it is from this that the principle of the Pythagorean philosophers was derived, who said, "He said it," speaking of their master in a glorious manner, since they feared to speak of him by name. And the same custom has obtained in cities and in private houses; for the servants, when speaking of the arrival of their master, say, "Here he comes;" and so when the prince of any individual city arrives, they use the same form of speech, "He comes," when they speak of him. But what is the purpose of this prolix enumeration of all these instances on my part? The truth is, that I wished to show that it is the Father of the universe who is spoken of here; since, indeed, all his good qualities, and all his marvellous names, are widely celebrated by the praise bestowed upon the virtues; and, therefore, out of reverence he has used that name more cautiously, because he was about to bring on the world the destruction of the flood; but the case of the pronoun "He" is used by way of honour in these phrases. "All flesh had corrupted His ways," inasmuch as it is truly convicted of having corrupted the way of the Father, in accordance with the lusts, and desires, and pleasures of the body; for these are the enemies and opposers of the laws of continence, and parsimony, and chastity, and fortitude, and justice; by which the road which leads to God is found out and widened, so that it should everywhere be a beaten and plain road.

(100) What is the meaning of the statement, "All the time of man has come against me, because the earth is filled with iniquity?" (Genesis 6:13).{14}{the version given here does not in the least resemble that in our Bible.} Those who resist the order of fate proceed upon these and many other arguments, especially in that of sudden death, which oftentimes produces great slaughter in a short period of time; as, for instance, in the overthrow of houses, in conflagrations, in shipwrecks, in civil tumults, in battles of cavalry, in wars by land and in wars by sea, and in pestilences. To all those who advance arguments of this kind we repeat the same assertions which are here made by the prophet, on the principle which is derived from himself. If indeed that expression, "All the time of man has come against me," has a meaning of this kind, the term which has been determined as the period of living for all mankind, behold it is now brought to one point and terminated at once by the deluge; and since this is the case, they will not live any longer according to the principle of fate which has been fixed; so that the time of each separate individual is now reduced to one, and has received its destined termination at the same time, by I know not what harmony and periodical revolution of the stars, by which bodies the whole race of mankind is continually preserved or destroyed. Let those, therefore, all receive these things in any manner in which they choose who study these things, and those too who argue against them. Nevertheless we must first of all make this statement, that nothing can be found so contrary to, so opposite to, so wholly repugnant to, the wonderful virtue of the Deity as iniquity; therefore, after he said, "All the time of all mankind has come up against me," he adds also the reason of its contrariety to him, that the earth is filled with iniquity. In the second place, Time, under the name of Chronos or Saturn, is looked upon as a god by the wickedest of men, who are desirous to lose sight of the one essential Being, on which account he says, "The time of all mankind has come up against me," because in fact the heathen make human time into a god, and oppose him to the real true God. But, however, it is now insinuated, in other passages also of scripture, which run thus, "Time has departed to a distance from them, but the Lord is in Us:"{15}{Numbers 14:9. Compare with this Isaiah 8, Jeremiah 46:21 - 28, Psalm 80:16.} just as if he were to say, time is looked upon by wicked men as the cause of the world, but by wise men and virtuous men time is not looked upon in this light, but God only, from whom all times and seasons do proceed. Again, God is the cause, not of all things, but only of good things and good men, and of those men and things which are in accordance with virtue; for as he is free from all wickedness, so likewise he cannot be the cause of it. In the third place, by that expression which he uses in this manner, he indicates the excess of impiety, saying, "that the time of all mankind has arrived," that is to say, that all men, in every part of the world, have agreed together, with one mind, to work wickedness; but the other assertion which is here made, that the whole earth is filled with iniquity, amounts to this, that there is no part of it whatever free from wickedness, and which is also to receive and to bear righteousness. And the expression, "against me," establishes the proof of what has been said, inasmuch as it is only the judgment of divine election which is altogether firm and lasting.

(1) What is the preparation of Noah? (Genesis 6:14). If any one should wish to make an examination of the question of that ark of Noah's on more natural principles, he will find it to have been the preparation of the human body, as we shall see by the examination of each particular respecting it separately.
(2) Why does he make the ark of squared pieces of wood? (Genesis 6:16). He does this in the first place, because the figure of a square, wherever it may be placed, is steady and firm, consisting as it does of right angles, and it is confirmed in a purer and clearer manner by the nature of the human body. In the second place, he does this because, although our body is an instrument, and although every portion of it is rounded off, nevertheless the limbs which are compounded of all these portions do, by some manner or other, evidently reduce that circular orb to the figure of a quadrangle or square. For example, take the breast which is rather square than circular; in the same manner take the belly, after it is swollen with food or by any natural excess, for there are some men potbellied by nature, who are to be excepted from our present argument. But if any one looks upon the arms and hands, and back and thighs, and feet of a man, he will find all these limbs compounded of a mixture of the square, with the circular figure at the same time. In the third place, a quadrangular piece of wood shows in its extension nearly every sort imaginable of uneven distinction, inasmuch as its length is greater than its breadth, and its breadth greater than its depth. And such also is the formation of our bodies, which are compounded of one extension which is great, of another which is of moderate size, of another which is small, great in its length and small in its depth.
(3) Why does God say, you shall make the ark in nests? (Genesis 6:14).{1}{the word in our Bible is rooms, not nests.} He gives this order very naturally, for the human body is formed of holes like nests; every one of which is nourished and grows like a young bird, a certain spiritual force which exists in it from its earliest origin penetrating through it, as, for instance, some of the holes and nests are the eyes, in which the faculty of sight has its abode; other nests are the ears, which are the place where hearing is situated. A third class of nests are the nostrils, in which the sense of smell is lodged. The fourth nest, which is of larger dimensions than those already mentioned, is the mouth, which is the seat of the taste; and it has been made of large size, since, besides taste, there is also another still more important instrument, which is that of articulate speech, reposing in it, namely, the tongue, which, as Socrates was wont to say, by beating in every direction in various manners, and by touching different parts, composes and forms a word, being, in truth, an instrument under the immediate guidance of reason. And the nest is placed under the skull, and that which is called the membrane of the brain is a certain nest, as it were, of the genius of each man: as also the chest is a nest, in which abide the lungs and the heart, and both these things are receptacles of other internal organs; the lungs being the place in which the power of breathing is lodged, and the heart being

the abode of both the blood and the breath, for it has two ventricles, which are, as it were, a certain kind of nests or receptacles in the breast; blood, from which the veins, as if they could perceive its operations, are irrigated; and a breathing-hole, which again is extended over and irrigates the perceptive channels of respiration. And both the harder as well as the softer parts do, like nests prepared for the purpose, nourish the bones as real nests nourish young birds; the harder portion of which, namely, the marrow, is the nest, and the softer flesh is the nest of pleasure and pain; and if any one should wish to investigate the other parts, he will find that, in every respect, the nature of man has much the same foundation as the ark.

(4) Why does God command the ark to be smeared with pitch, both on the inside and on the outside? (Genesis 6:14). Pitch is so called by reason of its bird-lime like tenacity, because it glues together whatever was disunited before, so as to form one indissoluble and indivisible joint. For everything which is held together by bird-lime is immediately held to a natural union; but our body being composed of many parts is united on the outside, and is held together by its own proper habit, but the previous habit of connection which binds those things together is the soul, which, being situated in the middle, penetrates through every part till it reaches the surface, and then is turned back again from the surface to the centre, so that our spiritual nature is rolled up compactly in a double fold, being united in a firm solidity and union. Therefore this ark is smeared with pitch, both on the inside and the outside, for the reason here given. But that ark which is placed in the holy of holies, and as covered over with gold, is the similitude of the world appreciable only by the intellect, as is declared in the account given of it: since just as there is a world appreciable by the intellect incarnate in incorporeal figures existing at the same time, consisting of a union of all figures by a certain invisible harmony; for, in proportion as gold is a more noble material than pitch, in the same ratio is that ark, which is in the holy of holies, superior to this one of which we are now speaking. And again, God ordained that its measure should be quadrangular, from a regard to usefulness; but his object in the other ark was not so much that it should be useful as that it should be exempt from all possibility of decay; for the nature of incorporeal things, appreciable only by the intellect, is to be exempt from decay, being incorruptible and permanent. The one ark is tossed to and fro by the winds and the waters, but the other has its station constantly in the holy of holies; and being stable it is akin to divine nature, as the other, which is tossed about in every direction, and moved from one place to another, is akin to and the emblem of created nature. Besides this, that ark of the flood being, as it were, an example of corruption, is raised on high, but the other, which is in the holy of holies, imitates the incorruptible condition of eternity.

(5) Why did God give the measures of the ark in the following manner; the length to be of three hundred cubits, and the breadth thereof to be fifty cubits, and the height to be thirty cubits: and above it was to be raised to a point in one cubit, being brought together gradually like an obelisk? (Genesis 6:15). It was necessary that so vast a work should be constructed in conformity with literal directions, in order that so many animals, some of them of vast size, should be received into it, as individuals of each class were introduced with the food necessary for them; but if the matter is considered properly with reference to its symbolical meaning, then, for the comprehension of the formation of our body, we shall require to make use not of the quantity of cubits, but of the certain principles and proportions which are observed in them. But the proportions which are contained in them are of sixfold, and double, and other portions are added. For three hundred is six times as many as fifty, and ten times as many as thirty; and again fifty is by two thirds a larger number than thirty. Such then are also the proportions of the body; for if any one should choose to investigate the matter and inquire into it carefully in all its points, he will find that man is made in an exact proportion of measurement, neither being too long or too little; and if a string be let down from his head to his feet, he will find that to reach that distance it requires a string six times as long as the width of his chest, and ten times as long as the depth of his ribs and their breadth as a second part of depth added thereto. Such is the certain proportion, received in accordance with nature, of the human body formed on exact measurement of the most excellently made men, who are incorrect neither in the way of excess nor of defect. But again, it was with great wisdom and propriety that God ordained the summit to be completed in one cubit; for the upper part of the ark imitates the unity of the body; the head being forsooth as the citadel of the king, having for its inhabitant the chief of all, the intellect. But those parts which are below the head are divided into separate portions, as for instance into the hands, and in an especial degree into the lower parts, since the thighs, and legs, and feet are all kept distinct from one another, therefore whoever should wish to understand these matters, on the principle which I have pointed out, will easily comprehend the analogy of the cubits as I have related it. But above all things he must not be ignorant that each of these different numbers of cubits has separately a certain necessary proportion and principle, beginning with the first, those in the length of the ark. Therefore in its length it is composed of three hundred units, placed next to one another in continuation, according to the augmentation of units, from these twenty-four numbers, one, two, three, four, five, six, seven, eight, nine, ten, eleven, twelve, thirteen, fourteen, fifteen, sixteen, seventeen, eighteen, nineteen, twenty, twentyone, twenty-two, twenty-three, twenty-four. But the twenty-fourth number is above all others a natural number, being distributed among the hours of day and night, and also among the characters of language, {2}{he is referring to the Greek alphabet, which consists of twenty-four letters.} and literal speech; and it is also compounded of three cubes, being complete, full, and compacted in equality. For the number three constantly exhibits, as belonging to itself, the first equality of all, having a beginning, and a middle, and an end, all of which are equal to one another; and eight is the first cube, because it again has declared its first equality with the rest. But the number twenty-four has likewise a great number of other virtues, since it is the substance of the number three hundred, as has been already pointed out; this then is its first virtue; and it has another, since it is compounded of twelve quadrangular figures, joined to one another by a continuous unity; and besides of two long figures, and twelve double figures, being forsooth compounded of twos separately increased by two and two. Therefore the angular numbers which make up together the twelve quadrangular figures are these; one, three, five, seven, nine, eleven, thirteen, fifteen, seventeen, nineteen, twenty-one, and twenty-three; but the quadrangular figure combines the following numbers, one, four, nine, sixteen, twenty-five, thirty-six, forty-nine, sixty-four, eighty-one, a hundred, a hundred and twenty-one, and a hundred and twenty-four. But those angular numbers which compose the other long figures are these; one, four, six, eight, ten twelve, fourteen, sixteen, eighteen, twenty, twenty-two, twenty-four, being twelve in all; and after these come the compound numbers, two, six, twelve, twenty, thirty, forty-two, fifty-six, seventy-two, ninety, a hundred and ten, a hundred and thirty-two, and a hundred and fifty-six; being also twelve. And if you put together the twelve quadrangular figures, you will find a hundred and forty-four, and if you add the other twelve long figures, you will find a hundred and fifty-six; and from the combination of the two you will get the number three hundred, and the concord of full, and complete, and perfect nature rising up to the equal and infinite harmony; for a complete and perfect nature is the maker of equality, according to the nature of a triangle; but the equal and the infinite are the factors of inequality, according to the composition of the other long figure. But the universe consists of a combination of equality and inequality, on which account the Creator himself, even amid the destruction of all earthly things, placed a sort of fixed pattern of stability in the ark. This then is enough to say about the number three hundred. We must now proceed to speak of the fifty cubits, on the following principle; for in the first place it is composed of the right angle of the quadrangular figures; for a right angle is compounded of three, four, and five; and the square of these is nine, sixteen, and twenty-five, the sum total of which when added together is fifty, In the second place, the perfect number fifty is composed of these four triangles linked together, one, three, six, ten; and again of these four equal quadrangles also united together, one, four, nine, sixteen; therefore these triangles when collected together make twenty; and the quadrangles make thirty; and twenty and thirty added together make fifty. But if the triangle and the quadrangle are added together, they make a heptangular figure: so that it is contained by its virtue in the number of fifty, that divine and holy number; to which the prophet had regard when he proclaimed the jubilee festival; and the whole of the jubilee year is free and a deliverer. The third theorem is three triangles beginning with the unit, connected together in a continuous series, and three cubes beginning also with the unit, and connected together in a similar manner, which together make fifty; the examples of the first are one, four, and nine, which make fourteen; the examples of the second are, one, eight, and twenty-seven, which together make thirty-six; and the sum total of the two when added together is fifty. Again, thirty is in an especial manner a natural number, for as in the series of units the number three is, so is the number thirty in the series of decimals; and that makes up the cycle of the moon, being the collection of separate months in full delineation; secondly, it is composed of four numbers, which are united in the continual series of these quadrangular figures, one, four, nine, and sixteen, which together make up thirty; on which account it was not without some foundation and sufficient reason that Heraclitus called that number "generation," when he said: a man in thirty years from the time of his birth can become a grandfather, inasmuch as he arrives at the age of puberty in his fourteenth year, at which age he is capable of becoming a father; and at the end of the year his offspring arrives at the birth, and again in fifteen years more begets another offspring like himself; and out of these names of grandfathers, fathers, and sons, as also out of the names of grandmothers, mothers, and daughters, a generation complete in its offspring is produced.

(6) What is the meaning of a door in the side: for he says, "Thou shalt make a door in the side?" (Genesis 6:16). That door in the side very plainly betokens a human building, which he has becomingly indicated by calling it, "in the side," by which door all the excrements of dung are cast out. In truth, as Socrates says, whether because he learnt it from Moses or because he was influenced by the facts themselves, the Creator, having due regard to the decency of our body, has placed the exit and passage of the different ducts of the body back out of the reach of the sense, in order that while getting rid of the fetid portions of bile, we might not be disgusted by beholding the full appearance of our excrements. Therefore he has surrounded that passage by the back and posteriors, which project out like hills, as also the buttocks are made soft for other objects.

(7) Why has he said that the lower part of the ark was to be made with two and with three stories? (Genesis 6:16). He has here admirably indicated the receptacles of food, calling them the inner parts of the house; since food is corruptible, and what is corruptible belongs to the inward part, because it is borne downwards, since some small portions of meat and drink which we take are borne upwards, but the greater part is secreted and cast out into dung; and the intestines have been made in two and in three stories, because of the providence of the Creator in order to supply abundant support to his creatures; for if he had made the receptacles of food and its passage having a direct communication between the bowels and the buttocks, some awkward circumstances must have taken place; in the first place there would have been a frequent deficiency, and want and hunger, and sudden evacuations also arising from divers unseasonable events; in the second place there would have been an immense hunger, for when the receptacles are emptied, it is inevitable that hunger and thirst must immediately supervene, like absolute mistresses in difficulty from pregnancy, and then it follows also that the pleasant appetite for food must be perverted into greediness and into an unphilosophical state; for nothing is so very inconvenient as for the belly to be empty. And in the third place, there will be death waiting at the door; since those persons must speedily be overtaken by death who the very moment that they have done eating begin again to be hungry, and the moment that they have drunk are again thirsty, and who before they are thoroughly filled are again evacuated and oppressed by hunger; but owing to the long coils and windings of the bowels we are delivered from all feelings of hunger, from all greediness, and from being prematurely overtaken by death; for while the food which has been taken remains within us, not for such a time only as the distance to be passed requires, but for so long as was necessary for us, a change in it is effected; since by the pressure to which it is subjected, the strength of the food is extracted in the first instance in the belly; then it is armed in the liver, and drawn out; after that whatever predominant flavour there was is emitted upwards to the separate parts, in the case of boys in order to contribute to their growth, and in the case of full grown men to add to their strength; and then nature, collecting the remaining portions into dung and excrement, casts them out. Therefore a great deal of time is necessarily required for the arrangement of so many and such important affairs, nature effecting its operations without difficulty by perseverance. Moreover the ark itself appears to me to be very fitly compared to the human body; for as nature is exceedingly prolific of living creatures, for that very reason it has prepared an opposite receptacle similar to the earth for the creatures corrupted and destroyed by the flood; for whatever was alive and supported on the earth, the ark now bore within itself in a more general manner, and on that account God ordained it, being borne upon the waters as it was, to be as it were like the earth, a mother and a nurse, and to exhibit the fathers of the subsequent race as if pregnant with it, together with the sun and moon, and the remaining multitude of the stars, and all the host of heaven; because men beholding by means of that which was made by art, a comparison and analogy to the human body, might in that manner be more manifestly taught, for this was the cause of the various disputes among mankind; since there is nothing which has so much contributed to keep man in a servile condition as the essential humours of the body, and the defects which arise in consequence of them, and most especially the vicious pleasures and desires.

(8) Why does he say that the deluge will be to the corrupting of all flesh in which there is the breath of life beneath the heaven? (Genesis 6:17). One may almost say that what he had previously spoken in riddles he has now made plain; for there was no other cause for the corruption of mankind, except that, being slaves to pleasure and to desire, they did everything, and were anxious about everything for that reason only; moreover they passed a life of extreme misery. But he added also, in a very natural manner, the place where the breath of life is, using the expression, "under heaven," because forsooth there are living beings also in heaven; for a happy body has not been made out of a heavenly substance, as if in truth it had received some peculiar and admirable condition, superior to that of other living creatures, but heaven appears to have been made especially worthy of and for the sake of these admirable and divine living beings, all of which are intellectual spirits; so that they give a share and participation in themselves and in the essence of vitality even to the creatures which exist upon the earth, and give life to all those which are capable of receiving it.

(9) Why does he say, all things which existed upon the earth shall be consumed; for what sin can the beasts commit? (Genesis 6:13). In the first place, as, when a sovereign is slain in battle the military valour of the kingdom is also crushed, so also he now has thought it reasonable that when the whole human race, bearing analogy to a sovereign, is destroyed, he should also destroy simultaneously with it the species of beasts likewise, on which account also in pestilences the beasts die first, and especially those which are bred up with and associate with men, such as dogs and similar animals, and afterwards the men die too. In the second place, as, when the head is cut off, no one blames nature if the other portions of the body also, numerous and important as they are, are destroyed along with it, so too now no one can find fault with anything, since man is as it were the head and chief of all animals, and when he is destroyed it is not at all strange if all the rest of the beasts are destroyed also along with him. In the third place, animals were originally made, not for their own sakes, as has been said by the philosophers, but in order to do service to mankind, and for their use and glory; therefore it is very reasonable that when those beings are destroyed for the sake of whom they had their existence, they also should be deprived of life, and this is the reason of this assertion in its literal sense; but with respect to its hidden meaning we may say, when the soul is exposed to a deluge from the overflow of vices, and is in a manner stifled by them, those portions also which are on the earth, the earthly parts I mean of the body, must of necessity likewise perish along with it; for life passed in wickedness is death; the eyes though they see perish, inasmuch as they see wrongly; the ears also though they hear perish, inasmuch as they hear wrongly; and the whole body of the senses perishes, inasmuch as they are all exercised wrongly.

(10) What is the meaning of the expression, I will set up my treaty with you? (Genesis 6:9). In the first place, he here warns us that no man is the inheritor of the divine substance, except him who is endowed with virtue; since the inheritance of men is possessed when they themselves are no longer in existence, but when they are dead; but as God is everlasting he grants a participation in his inheritance to wise men, rejoicing at their entering into possession of it; for he who has entered into possession of everything is in want of nothing, but they who are in distress from a want of all things are in the possession of no portion of truth. And on this account God, showing himself favourable to the virtuous, benefits them, bestowing on the those things of which they have need. In the second place, he bestows on the wise man a certain and more ample inheritance; for he does not say, I will set up my treaty for you, but with you; that is to say, you are yourself a just and true treaty, which I will set up for the race endued with reason, who have need of virtue, for a possession and a glory to them.

(11) Why does he say: "Enter thou and all thy house into the ark, because I have seen that thou art a just man before me in that generation?" (Genesis 7:1). In the first place, certain faith receives approbation, inasmuch as for the sake of one man who is just and worthy many men are saved by reason of their relationship to him; as is the case too with sailors and armies, when the one have a good captain and the others an excellent and skilful general. In the second place, he extols the just man with praise, who thus acquires virtues, not for himself alone, but also for his whole family, which in this way deserves safety. And it is with peculiar propriety that this expression is added, namely, "I have seen that thou art a just man before me;" for men approve of the life of any one upon one principle, and God on quite a different one; for they judge by what is visible, but he derives his tests from the invisible designs of the soul. Moreover, that is a very remarkable expression which is added as an insertion, namely, the one which says, "I have seen that thou art a just man in this generation;" that he might not appear to condemn those who had gone before, nor cut off the future hope of coming generations. This is the sense of the passage taken according to the letter. But if we look at its inward meaning, when God will save the intellect of the soul, which is the principal part of the man, that is to say, the head of the family, then also he will save the whole family along with him; I mean all the parts, and all those who bear an analogy to the parts, and to the word which is uttered, and to the circumstances of the body; for what the intellect is in the soul, that also is the soul in the body. All the parts of the soul are in good condition, owing to the result of counsels, and all its family derives the benefit along with it. But when the whole soul is in a good condition, then also its habitation is again found to be benefited by purity of morals and sobriety, those overstrained desires which are the causes of diseases being cut off.

(12) Why does he order seven of each of the clean animals, male and female, to be taken into the ark, but of the unclean animals only two, male and female, in order to preserve seed upon all the earth? (Genesis 7:2). By divine ordinance he has asserted the number seven to be clean, and the number two to be unclean; since the number seven is clean by nature, inasmuch as that is a virgin number, free from all admixture, and without any parent. Nor does it generate any thing, nor is it generated, as each of those numbers which are below the number ten, on account of their similitude to the unit, because it is uncreated and unbegotten, and nothing is generated by it, although it is itself the cause of creation and generation; because it rouses the virtues of all things which are well-arranged, for the generation of created beings. But the number two is not clean. In the first place, because it is empty, not solid; and because it is not full, therefore neither is it clean; because it is likewise the beginning of infinite immensity by reason of its materiality. It also labours under inequality on account of the other long numbers; for all the other numbers after two which are increased in a twofold proportion are long numbers. But that which is unequal is not clean, as neither is that which is material; but that which proceeds from such is fallible and inelegant, being destitute of the purity of reason to conduct it to completeness and perfection; and it conducts it to such by its own intrinsic power, and by songs of harmony and equality. This is enough to say on the physical part of the subject; it remains for us to speak of its moral bearings. The irrational parts of our soul which are destitute of intellect are divided into seven; that is to say, into the five senses, and the vocal organ, and the seminal organ. Now these in a man endued with virtue are all clean, and by nature feminine, inasmuch as they belong to the irrational species; but to a man who has come into full possession of his inheritance they are masculine; for men endued with virtue are also the parents of the virtue of counsel to themselves, the best part of them not permitting them to come to the external senses in a precipitate and unbridled manner, but repressing them and leading them back to right reason. But in the wicked man there exists a twofold wickedness; since the injust man is full of doubts and perplexities, as a hesitating person, mingling things which ought not to be mixed, and connecting them with one another, confounding those things which may very easily be kept separate. Such are those passions which imbue the soul with some particular colour, like a man spotted and leprous in body, the originally sound counsel being infected and contaminated by that which is destructive and fatal. But the principle of the entrance and of the custody of animals is added in a natural manner; for he says, "for the sake of nourishing seed." If we take the expression according to the letter, inasmuch as, although particular individuals may be destroyed, still at least a race is preserved to be the seed of future generations; forsooth that the intention of God, conceived at the formation of the world, might remain for ever and ever unextinguishable, the different races of creatures being preserved. But if we regard the inward meaning of the words, it is necessary that in the irrational parts of the soul, likewise, there should be motions which are clean, as certain seminal principles, although the animals themselves are not clean; since the nature of mankind is capable of admitting contrarieties, for instance, virtue and wickedness; each of which he delineated at the creation of the world, by the tree bearing the name of the tree of knowledge of good and evil. Forsooth our intellect, in which there is both knowledge and intelligence, comprehends both good and evil; but good is akin to the number seven, and evil is the brother of duality. Moreover, the law of wisdom, which abounds in beauty, says expressly and carefully, that seed is to be nourished, not in one place only, but in all the earth, both naturally, in the first instance, and also morally, in its peculiar sense; because it is very natural, and suitable to the character of God, to cause that which in all parts and divisions of the world is said again to be the seed of living beings, to fill places which have been evacuated a second time with similar creatures, by a repeated generation; and not altogether to desert our body, inasmuch as it is an earthly substance, as if it were a thing deserted by and void of all principle of life. Since, if we practise the drinking of wines and the eating of meats, and indulge in the ardent desire of the female, and in short practise in all things a delicate and luxurious life, we are then only the bearers of a corpse in the body; but if God, taking compassion on us, turns away the overflow of vices and renders the soul dry, he will then begin to make the body living, and to animate it with a purer soul, the governing principle of which is wisdom.

(13) Why, after the entrance of Noah into the ark, did seven days elapse, after which the deluge came? (Genesis 7:10). The kind Saviour of the world allows a space for the repentance of sinners, in order that when they see the ark placed in front of them as a sort of type, made with respect to the then present time, and when they see all the different kinds of living creatures shut up in it which the earth used to bear on its surface, according to its parts adapted to the different species, they might believe the predictions of the deluge which had been made to them, so that, fearing total destruction above all things, they might be speedily converted, destroying and eradicating all their iniquity and wickedness. In the second place, this language is a most manifest representation of the exceeding great abundance of the kind mercy of the beneficent Saviour, by destroying the wickedness of many years, which from the time of their birth to old age has extended itself over their conduct in those persons who practise penitence for a few days, for the divine nature forgets all evil and is a lover of virtue. When therefore it beholds faithful virtue in the soul, it gives it honour in a wonderful degree, in order, in the first place, to take away all kinds of evil which impend over it from its sins. In the third place, the number of seven days after the entrance of Noah into the ark, during which the command of God kept off the flood, is a recollection of the creation of the world, the birthday festival of which is kept on the seventh day, showing manifestly the authority of the Father; just as if he were to say, "I am the Creator of the world, commanding things to exist which have no existence; and at the same time I am he who am now about to destroy the world with a great flood. But the original cause of the creation of the world was the goodness which is in me, and my kindness; and the cause of its impending destruction is the ingratitude and impiety of those persons who have been loaded by benefits by me." Therefore he causes an interval of seven days, in order that the unbelieving may remember, and that those who have abandoned their faith in the Parent of the world may in a suppliant spirit return to the Creator of all things, and so may entreat him again that his works may be everlasting; and that they may offer their entreaty, not with mouth and tongue, but rather with the heart of amendment and penitence.

(14) Why did the rain of the deluge last forty days and an equal number of nights? (Genesis 7:4). In the first place, the word day is used in a double sense. The one meaning that time which is from morning to evening, that is to say, from the first rising of the sun in the east to his sinking in the west. Therefore they who make definitions, say, "That is day, as long as the sun shines on the earth." In another sense, the word day is used of the day and night together. And in this sense we say that a month consists of thirty days, combining together and computing the period of night in the same calculation. These premises having been first laid down thus, I say that the word now spoken of has not been incorrectly employed, inasmuch as it implies forty days and forty nights; but is also so used in order to suggest a double number determined for the generation of mankind, namely, forty and eighty, as many men skilled in medicine, and indeed also in physical science, have suggested; but it is especially described in the sacred law, which was to them also the first principle of natural science. Since therefore destruction was on the point of overwhelming all men and women every where on account of the excessive combination of iniquities and quarrels, the Judge of all considered it becoming to allot an equal time to their destruction to that which he had consumed in the original creation of nature and to the work of giving life to the world; for the principle of procreation is the perseverance of seed in the different parts; but it was necessary to honour the male creature with pure light, which knows not the shade; but the woman had a mixture in her body of night and darkness. Therefore, in the creation of the whole world, the excess of the male or the unequal number, being composed of unity, becomes the parent of square numbers; but the woman who is an unequal number, being compounded of duality, becomes the parent of other long numbers. Moreover, the square is splendour and light combining together by the equality of the sides; but the other numbers being long necessarily exhibit night and darkness by reason of their inequality, since that which is in excess throws a shade over that which lies beneath the excess. In the second place, the number forty is the produce of many virtues, as has been suggested in another place. It is also often used for the judgment of legislation, both with reference to those persons who have done any thing rightly deserving of praise and honour, and also with reference to those who on account of their sins meet with reproaches and punishments; so that it is superfluous to adduce proofs to demonstrate what is evident.

(15) What is the meaning of the expression, "I will destroy every living substance that I have made form off the face of the earth?" (Genesis 7:4). Do you not all shrink back in astonishment when you hear these words, by reason of the beauty of the sentence? for he has not said, "destroy from the earth," but "from the face of the earth," that is to say from its surface; in order, that is, that in the lowest depth of the earth the vital efficacy of all seeds might be preserved unhurt, and free from all injury which could possibly bring damage to it; since the Creator was not forgetful of his original design, but destroys those only who come in his way, and who move only on the surface of the earth, but leaves the roots in the depth, in order to produce the generation of other causes. Moreover, that expression, "I will destroy," was also written by divine inspiration; for it happens that if we remove the letters which require to be removed, the whole table for the reception of letters remains the same. By which he proves that he will destroy the fickle generation on account of their impiety, but the conversation and essence of the human race he will preserve for ever and ever to be the seed of future generations. And what follows agrees with this, since to the expression, "I will destroy," this other is also added, all natural existence, every thing which exists, or rises upon the earth; but existence is the destruction of the opposite characteristics; and that which is dissolved loses quality, but retains body and materiality. This is the letter of what is said. But in the inward meaning, the flood is symbolically representative of spiritual dissolution. When therefore by the grace of the Father we desire to throw away and to wash off all sensible and corporeal qualities by which the intellect was infected as by swelling sores, then the muddy slime is got rid of as by a deluge, sweet waters and wholesome fountains supervening.

(16) Why does he say: "Noah did every thing which the Lord commanded (or ordered) him?" (Genesis 7:5). A noble panegyric for the just man. In the first place, because with an ingenuous mind and a purpose full of affection towards God he performed, not a part of what he had been commanded, but the whole of God's commands. But the second is the more true expression, because he does not choose so much to command as to order him; for masters command their slaves, but friends order friends, and especially elder friends order younger ones. Therefore it is a marvellous gift to be found even in the rank of servants, and in the list of ministers of God; and it is a superabundant excess of kindness for any one to be a beloved friend to the most glorious Uncreated Essence. Moreover, the sacred writer has here carefully employed both names, the Lord God, as declaratory of his superior powers of destroying and benefiting, using the word Lord first, and placing the name God, giving the idea of beneficence, second; since it was a time of judgment let the name which is the indication of his destroying power come first. But still, as he is a kind and merciful king, he leaves as relics the seminal elements by which the vacant places may be replenished, for which reason, at the fist beginning of the account of the creation, the expression, "Let there be," was not an exterminating act of power, but a beneficent one. Therefore, at the creation, he changed the appellations and use of names; but as the name God is an indication of his beneficent power, the sacred writer has more frequently employed that in his account of the creation of the universe, but after everything was perfected then he called him Lord, in reference to the creation itself, for this name betokens royal power and the ability to destroy; since, where the act of generation is God is used first in order, but when punishment is spoken of the name Lord is placed before the name God.

(17) Why did the deluge take place in the six hundredth year of the life of Noah, and in the seventh month, and on the twenty-seventh day of the month? (Genesis 7:11). Perhaps it happened that the just man was born at the beginning of the month, at the first beginning of the commencement of that very year which they are accustomed to call the sacred year, out of honour, otherwise the sacred historian would not have been so carefully accurate in fixing the day and month when the deluge began to the seventh month and the twenty-seventh day of the month. But, perhaps, by this minuteness he intended manifestly to indicate the precise time of the vernal equinox, for that always occurs on the twenty-seventy day of the seventh month. But why was it that the deluge fell on the day of the vernal equinox? Because about that time the birth and increase of everything take place, whether living creatures or plants; therefore the vengeance and punishment inflicted brings with it the more terrible and dreadful threats, as happening at the period of plenty and fertility of the shaves of corn, and indeed, in the very midst of that productiveness, and bringing the evil of utter destruction as a reproof of the impiety of those who are exposed to the punishment. For behold, says he, all nature contains its own productions within itself in the greatest abundance, namely, wheat and barley, and everything else which is produced from seed, brought on to complete generation, as, also, it begins to generate the fruits of trees; but you, like mortals, corrupt its mercies, perverting the divine gifts, and purposes, and mysteries. But if the deluge had taken place at the autumnal equinox, when there was nothing growing on the earth, but when all the crops were collected into their proper storehouses, it would not have, in any degree, been looked upon as a punishment, but rather as a benefit, as the water would have cleansed the plains and the mountains. But as the first man who was produced out of the earth was also created at the same season of the year, he whom the divine writer calls Adam, because in fact it was on every account proper that the grandfather, or original parent, or father of the human race, or by whatever name we may choose to designate that original founder of our kind, should be created at the season of the vernal equinox, when all earthly productions were full of their fruit; but the vernal equinox takes place in the seventh month, which is also called the first in other passages, with reference to a different idea. Since, therefore, the first beginning of the generation of our race, after the destruction caused by the deluge, commenced with Noah, men being again sown and procreated, therefore he also is recognised as resembling the first man born of the earth, as far as such resemblance or recognition is possible. And the six hundredth year has for its origin the number six; and the world was created under the number six, therefore, by this same number does he reprove the wicked, putting them to shame because he would, unquestionably, never, after he had created the universe by means of the number six, have destroyed all the men who lived on the earth under the form of six, if it had not been for the preposterous excess of their iniquities. For the third power of six and the minor power is the number six hundred, and the mean between both is sixty, since the number ten more evidently represents the likeness of unity, and the number a hundred represents the minor power.

(18) What is the meaning of the expression, "And the fountains of the deep were broken, and the springs of heaven were opened?" (Genesis 7:11). The literal meaning is plain enough, for it suggests the two extremities of the universe, the heaven and the earth, to have met together for the destruction of mortals deserving of condemnation, the waters running forth to meet one another from all quarters, for part of them bubbled up from out of the earth, and part descended downwards from heaven; and in truth, that expression is very explicit, "The fountains were broken up," for when a rupture is effected then the thing confined rushes forth without any hindrance. But with reference to the interior meaning of the expression we may as well say this: the heaven is symbolically the human intellect, and the earth is the sense and body, therefore there is great distress and calamity when neither remains, but when each threatens a secret attack. But what is the exact meaning of my words? If often happens that acuteness of intellect exhibits cunning and wickedness, and bears itself with bitterness in every respect when the lusts of the body are restrained and bridled; but the contrary fact often prevails, and the lusts rejoice in their opportunities and proceed onward, gaining strength from luxury and abundance of means; therefore, the gate of these lusts is the outward sense combined with the body; but when the intellect, neglecting outward circumstances, is consistent with itself, then the senses lie harmless, as if completely abandoned; but when both are united, the intellect in exerting all cunning and wickedness, and the body irrigated with all the senses and gorged with every kind of vice to satiety, then we are exposed to a deluge; and this is in fact a great deluge, when the streams of the intellect are opened by iniquity, and folly, and greedy desire, and injustice, and arrogance, and impiety, and when the fountains of the body are opened by lust, and desire, and intemperance, and obscenity, and gluttony, and lasciviousness, with relations and sisters, and all irremediable diseases.

(19) What is the meaning of the expression, "And the Lord shut him in, closing the doors of the ark?" (Genesis 7:16). Since we have said that the structure of the human body is symbolically indicated by the ark, we must take notice, also, that on the outside this body is enclosed by a hard and dense skin, to be a covering to all its parts; for nature has made this as a sort of coat, to prevent either cold or heat from being able to do man injury. The literal meaning of the expression is plain enough, for the door of the ark is carefully shut by divine

virtue for the sake of security, lest the water should enter in at any part, as it was to be tossed about by the waves for an entire year.
(20) What is the meaning of the expression, "And the water was greatly increased, and bore up the ark which floated upon the water?" (Genesis 7:17). The literal meaning is plain enough, but it contains an allegorical reference to our bodies, which ought to be borne up as if on the water, and by fluctuating with our necessities to subdue hunger and thirst, cold and heat, by which it is agitated, disturbed, and kept in motion.
(21) Why did the water overflow fifteen cubits above all the highest mountains? (Genesis 7:19). With respect to the literal statement we must remark that the excess was not merely one of fifteen cubits above all high mountains but above those which were a great deal more lofty and high than some others; therefore it was a great deal more than that height above the lower ones. But we must interpret this statement allegorically; for the loftier mountains shadow forth the senses in our body, because it has been permitted to them to occupy the abode of stability in the lofty region of our head. And there are five numbers of these, each to be considered separately, so that they amount in all to fifteen.
As, there is the faculty of sight, the thing which is visible, the act of seeing.
The faculty of hearing, the thing which is audible, and the act of hearing.
The faculty of smelling, the thing which can be smelled, and the act of smelling.
The faculty of taste, the thing which can be tasted, and the act of tasting.
The faculty of touch, the thing which can be touched, and the act of touching.
These are the fifteen cubits in excess; for they also are overwhelmed by the overflow, being destroyed by the unseasonable influx of infinite vices and evils.
(22) What is the meaning of the expression, "And all flesh capable of motion perished?" (Genesis 7:21). It is with especial propriety, and strictly in accordance with natural truth, that the sacred historian has here pronounced all flesh capable of motion devoted to destruction; for flesh excites pleasures, and is excited by pleasures; and such affections are the causes of the destruction of souls, as one the other hand sobriety and patience are the causes of safety.
(23) What is the meaning of the expression, "And everything which was on the dry land died?" (Genesis 7:22). The literal meaning is notorious, because in that great deluge everything which was upon the earth was destroyed and perished; but with respect to the secret meaning, as, since the material of timber, when it is parched and dry, is readily consumed by fire, so, likewise, when the soul is not mingled with wisdom, and justice, and piety, and the other enduring virtues, which alone are able to impart real joy to the thoughts, then it, being parched up and dried like a plant which is deprived of any power of budding or producing seed, or like a withered trunk, dies, being handed over to the mercy of the overwhelming overflow of the body.
(24) What is the meaning of the words, "It destroyed every living substance which was on the face of the earth?" (Genesis 7:23). The literal meaning of these words only announces a plain statement of a fact, but it may be turned into an

allegory in this manner. It is not without reason that the sacred historian has used the words "a living substance," for that is characteristic of ambition and pride, which lead men to despise both divine and human laws; but ambition and arrogance do rather appear on the face of our earthly and corporeal nature with an elated countenance and contracted brows. Since there are some persons who come nearer to one with their feet, but with their chests, and necks, and heads lean back, and are actually borne backwards and bend away like a balance, so that with one half of their body, in consequence of the position of their feet, they project forward, but backward with the upper portion of their chests, drawing themselves back like those persons whose muscles and nerves are in pain, by which they are prevented from stooping in a natural manner. But men of this kind it was determined to put an end to, as one may see from the records of the Lord and the divine history of the scriptures.

(25) What is the meaning of the words, "Noah remained alone, and they who were with him in the ark?" (Genesis 7:24). The literal meaning of this is evident; but with respect to its concealed sense we may advance an opinion, that the intellect which is desirous of studying justice and wisdom does, like a tree, discard all noxious shoots which bud forth about it, and rejects all extravagant humours of superfluous vigour, I mean immoderate excess of the affections, and wickedness, and all the effects of such. Therefore he is here said to have been left alone with those of his own kindred, and his kindred are properly all those designs and thoughts of each individual, which are regulated in accordance with virtue, on which account the statement is added "And he remained alone, and they who were with him," in order to reveal a more genuine joy; but he remained in the ark, that is to say, in the body, because it was purified from every vice and spiritual disease, as the intellect was not yet put in such a condition as to be wholly incorporeal. And on this account also, we must render thanks to the merciful Father, because he received his consort and colleague no longer as one endowed with superior power, but to be subordinate to his own power, on which account also the body is not submerged in the deluge, but rising above the flood is not at all destroyed by the eddies of the cataracts, which a crapulous, libidinous, vanity-loving will, overflowing all things, raises to an eminence.

(26) Why is it that the sacred writer says, "And God was mindful of Noah, and of the beasts, and of the cattle," but does not add that he remembered his wife and children? (Genesis 8:1). As the husband agrees with and is equal to his wife, and as the father is equal to his sons, there is no need of mentioning more names than one, but one, the first, is sufficient; therefore, by naming Noah he, in effect, names all those who were with him of his family; for when husband, and wife, and children, and relations are all agitated by discord, then it is no longer possible for such to be called one family, but instead of being one they are many; but when harmony exists then one family is exhibited by one superior of the house, and all are seen to depend upon that one, like the branches of a tree which shoot out from it, or the fruit upon a vine branch which does not fall off from it. And in another part, also, the prophet has said, "Have a regard to Abraham your father, and to Sarah who brought you forth," where, because in fact it was one family, he displays the agreement by mentioning the woman.

(27) Why is it that the sacred writer made mention first of the beasts and afterwards of the cattle, saying that God remembered Noah, and the beasts, and the cattle? (Genesis 8:1). In the first place, that poetical rule has not been expressed in vain, that he led the bad into the middle; therefore he places the beasts in the middle, between the domestic animals, that is to say the men and the cattle, in order that they might be tamed and civilized by having an intimate association with both. In the second place, he thought it scarcely reasonable to bestow a provident benefit on the beasts by themselves, because he was about immediately to add a statement of the beginning of the diminution of the deluge. This is the explanation of the statement taken literally. But with respect to the inner meaning, that just intellect, dwelling in the body as if in the ark, possesses both beasts and living animals, not those particular ones which bite and hurt, but, that I may use such an expression, those general kinds which contain in themselves the principles of seed and origination; since without these the soul cannot be manifest in the body. Moreover, the soul of the foolish man employs all poisonous and deadly animals, but that of the wise man those only which have changed the nature of wild beasts into that of domestic creatures.

(28) What is the meaning of the expression, "He brought a breath over the earth, and the water ceased?" (Genesis 8:2). Some people say that what is here meant by "a breath" is the wind, at which the deluge ceased. But I am not aware that water is diminished by wind, but only that it is disturbed and agitated into waves, for if it were otherwise the vast extent of the sea would have been wholly dried up long ago. Therefore it appears to me that the sacred writer here means the breath of the Deity, by which the whole universe obtains security at the same time with the calamities of the world, and with those things which exist in the air, and in every mixture of plants and animals. Since the deluge of that time was no trifling infliction of water, but an immense and boundless overflow, extending almost beyond the pillars of Hercules and the great Mediterranean Sea, since the whole earth and all the spaces of the mountains were covered with water; and it is scarcely likely that such a vast space could have been cleared by a wind, but rather, as I have said, it must have been done by some invisible and divine virtue.

(29) What is the meaning of the expression, "The fountains of the deep were closed, and the cataracts of heaven?" (Genesis 8:2). In the first place, it is agreed upon by all that in the first period of forty days the waters of punishment fell uninterruptedly, the lowest fountains of the earth being burst asunder; and from above, the cataracts of heaven being opened, and pouring down until all places, both level and mountainous, were covered with the inundation; and for another period of a hundred and fifty entire days the waters did not cease to fall, nor did the streams cease to flow, nor the springs to burst up, though still in milder quantities, not so as to increase the existing flood, but only so as to secure the duration of the existence of the deluge, which was also assisted from on high; and this is what is indicated in the meantime by the statement that after a hundred and fifty days the fountains and the cataracts were closed up; therefore, while as yet they were not closed up it is plain that they were in action. In the second place, it was necessary that that which afforded the excessive supply of waters for the deluge, namely, the double reservoir of water, the one from the fountains of the earth, and the other from the pourings forth of heaven, should be both closed, for the more the stores from which any material is supplied fail, the more it is consumed by itself, especially when divine virtue has given the command. This is the literal meaning of the expression. But with respect to the inner sense of the passage, since the deluge of the mind arises from two things, for it arises partly from counsel, as if from heaven, and in another degree also from the body and from sense, as if from earth, the vices being reciprocally introduced by the passions and the passions by the vices, it was inevitably necessary that the word of the divine physician entering in as a salutary visitation for the purpose of healing the disease, should prevent both kinds of overflow for the future; for it is the first principle of the medical art to drive away the cause of the infirmity and to leave no longer any materials for disease; and the scripture teaches this, also, in the case of the leper, for when the leprosy is checked and is prevented from extending further, it then fixes the station and abode of the leprous man in the same place by a law, because the character of being stationary implies cleanliness, for that which is moved contrary to nature is unclean.

(30) What is the meaning of the statement that after a hundred and fifty days the water began to abate? (Genesis 8:3). We must here inquire whether those hundred and fifty days, during which the water was abating, are to be distinguished from the four months, or whether they have a reference to the days previously mentioned, during which the deluge went on unceasingly, as still increasing.

(31) Why does he say, "The ark settled in the seventh month on the seven and twentieth day of the month?" (Genesis 8:4). It is reasonable here to consider how the beginning of the deluge commences in the seventh month, on the twenty-seventh day of the month, and how the diminution, when the ark rested on the top of the mountains, again took place in the seventh month and on the twenty-seventh day of the month; therefore we must say, that there is here an homonymy of months and days, for the beginning of the flood took place in the seventh month, beginning at the birthday of the just man, near the time of the vernal equinox, and its diminution took place in the seventh month, beginning from the highest point of the flood at the autumnal equinox, since the two equinoxes are separated from one another by seven months, having an interval of five months between them. For the seventh month of the equinox is also by its virtue the first month, because the creation of the world took place in it, on account of the abundance of all things at that season. And, in like manner, the seventh month of the autumnal equinox, which, according to time, is the first in dignity, having its principle of that number seven derived from the air; therefore, the deluge took place in the seventh month, not according to time but according to nature, having for its principle and commencement the spring season.

(32) Why does he say, "In the tenth month, on the first day of the month, the heads of the mountains appeared?" (Genesis 8:4). As in numerals the number ten is the extreme bound of the units, being a definitive and perfect number, so too it is the cycle and end of the units, and also the beginning and cycle of the decades, and of infinity of numbers; thus the Creator, on the cessation of the deluge, condescended that the tops of the mountains should appear in the number of the decade, being a definitive and perfect number.

(33) Why was it after forty days that the just man opened the window of the ark? (Genesis 8:5). We must observe carefully that the divine historian uses the same number in speaking of the influx of the deluge and in mentioning the cessation and complete removal of the evil; forsooth on the twenty-seventh day of the seventh month in the six hundredth year of the life of Noah, that is to say in the six hundredth year after his nativity, the deluge began at the spring season; but on the twenty-seventh day of the seventh month, the ark rested on the top of the mountains at the vernal equinox. But it is plain from these circumstances that the deluge became invisible in the six hundred and first year of Noah's life, again on the seventh month and the twenty-seventh day of it, so that after the lapse of an entire year, it again settled and established the earth as it was at the moment of its destruction, in the spring season, budding forth and covered with verdure and full of all kinds of fruits. But again in a similar manner the overflow of the deluge took place for forty days, the cataracts of heaven being opened and fountains bursting upwards from the lowest depths of the earth; and again a hope of renewal took place at intervals of forty days after a sufficient cessation of the rains, when he opened the window; and again the duration of the permanent deluge lasted for a period of a hundred and fifty days, as also its gradual diminution occupied a period of a hundred and fifty days; so that we may well admire the equality of the arrangement, for the evil increased and ceased according to the same number, like the moon, which from its first rise proceeds in its increase according to an equal number, going onward to its perfect fulness of light, and then again with an equal number in its decrease, returning back to its original state, after having been previously full; and in like manner in the case of divine chastisements, the Creator preserves a regular order, banishing all irregularity from the divine borders.

(34) What is the window of the ark, which the just man opens? (#Ge 8:6). The literal statement scarcely admits of any difficulty or doubt, inasmuch as it is plain; but with reference to the inner meaning we have this to say: each separate part of the senses has imitated the windows of the body, since it is through them as through windows that the comprehension of sensible objects enters into the intellect, and again it is through them that the intellect stretches forth as if escaping; but a portion of these windows, the senses, the more noble portion too, I say, is the sight; inasmuch as that above all the rest is akin to the soul, and it is intimately acquainted with light, the most beautiful of the essences, and it is the minister of sacred things; moreover that is the one which first laid open the road to philosophy. For beholding the regular motion of the sun, and of the moon, and the erratic course of the other planets, and the unerring circular motion of the whole heaven, and the order and harmony there existing beyond all calculation, as if it were the one real creator of the whole world, it by itself related to its one chief counsellor and director all that it saw: and then intellect, seeing those things with its acute eye, and by those things discerning superior demonstrative ideas, and the cause of all those things, immediately perceived that there was a God at the same moment that it arrived at the conception of generation and providence, because forsooth it was plain that this visible nature was not created by itself: for it was impossible that such a harmony, and order, and reason, and most consistent analogy, and that a concord of such a character and extent, and that such true and perfect felicity should exist by its own power: but it was necessary that there must be some Creator and parent of it acting like a governor and director, who generated these things, and then having generated them preserves them safe and sound.

(35) Why did he send out a raven first? (Genesis 8:6). If we look to the literal statement, the raven is said to be an animal particularly set apart for being sent on messages and employed in offices; for to this very day many people watch its mode of flight and its chattering, judging that it gives some intimation of unknown facts; but with respect to the hidden meaning, as a raven is a black, and arrogant, and speedy animal, it is a sign of wickedness, which brings night and darkness over the soul, and it is also swift to meet all the things of the world in its flight. And also that it is very bold, so as at times to cause the destruction of those who seek to catch it, since pride produces also rash impudence, the opposite of which is virtue, which is consistent with the brilliancy of light, and is by nature decorated with a modest bashfulness; therefore it is quite natural that if there was any darkness remaining behind in the intellect, darkness which exists in accordance with folly, he should expel that and send it out beyond his borders.

(36) Why did the raven after it had gone forth not return, when there was not yet any part of the earth dried? (Genesis 8:7). This passage admits of an allegorical interpretation since injustice is contrary to the light of justice; so that in comparison of the admirable actions of the man endued with virtue, it thinks it more desirable to rejoice with its kinsman the deluge; for injustice is a lover of confusion and corruption.

(37) Why does he speak here in an incorrect manner, "Till the water was dried up from the earth;" when it was not the water which was dried up from the earth, but the earth which was dried from the water? (Genesis 8:7). He uses this expression in an allegorical sense, indicating by the fall of the waters the immensity of vices, by which when saturated and vigorous the soul is corrupted, but when they are dried up and withered, it is preserved; for then they cannot inflict any mischief upon it, since they are become impotent and dead.

(38) Why does he in the second place send forth the dove, and why does he send it forth from himself to see whether the water had ceased, when he uses no such expressions about the raven? (Genesis 8:8). In the first place, the dove is a clean animal, and in the second place it is tame, civilised, and one which associates with mankind, on which account also the honour has been allotted to it of being offered up upon the altar in sacrifices; and on this account the sacred writer, sanctioning this honour and adding the weight of his assertion, has said, he sent it forth from himself, declaring by this expression that it was to see whether the water was abated, he displays the common anxiety felt by both. But those birds, the raven and the dove, are symbols of wickedness and virtue: for the one, whether it is wickedness or the raven, has no house, nor habitation, nor city, being an insolent unsociable bird; but the other, namely virtue, has a regard to humanity, and to the public good: and so the man endowed with virtue sends that bird forth as his ambassador for desirable and salutary objects, wishing to receive from it desirable information; and she, like an ambassador, brings us back genuine pleasure, so that what is hurtful may be guarded against, and what is useful may be diligently and carefully admitted.

(39) Why did the dove, when it found no rest for its feet, return to Noah? (Genesis 8:9). Is not the reason of this evident, and is it not a plain proof that wickedness and virtue are symbolically indicated by the raven and the dove? For behold the dove, which is the last sent out, finds no rest. How, then, could the raven, who departed previously, while the calamity of the deluge was still prevailing, find any place, and make a settlement? For the raven was neither a swan nor an ibis, nor did he belong to the class of aquatic birds. But the sacred writer here points out in an enigmatical manner, that wickedness, when it has gone forth out of doors, to the swelling whirlpools of the vices and passions which overflow and corrupt the soul and life, joyfully admits them, and dwells with and takes up its abode with them, as with its nearest friends and relations; but virtue, turning away with loathing from even the first sight of them, at once springs back, and does not return, scarcely finding rest for its feet; finding, in fact, no standing ground anywhere, and no place worthy of itself. For what other greater evil can there be than this, that virtue should not be able to find in the soul any place ever so small for rest and for abiding in?

(40) What is the meaning of the statement, "Putting forth his hand, he received her, and brought her in to himself?" (Genesis 8:9). The literal meaning is plain, but with respect to the hidden sense we must elicit the truth carefully. The wise man employs truth as an overseer of and ambassador in important affairs, which, when it perceives that those natures are worthy of it, abides among and dwells with them, correcting them, and making them better, since wisdom is a very common, and equal, and useful thing. But when, with reference to the opposite natures, it sees that in some points they are preposterously redundant and in others altogether deficient, it returns to its proper place; and the man endowed with virtue admits it in word, putting forth his hand to take it, and in fact opening all his intellect for its reception, and unfolding it by the perfect number, full and equal, with all imaginable promptitude. Nor even then, when he had sent her forth from himself to examine the natures of other things, had he separated it from himself, but had only acted like the sun, which sends forth his beams to give light to all things, because it is not at all consistent with the character of his boundless light to be separated at all.

(41) Why did he, after waiting yet seven other days, send forth the dove a second time? (Genesis 8:10). This is an excellent example for life, since although it will behold natures obstinate at first, still the hope of changing them into better natures is scarcely allowed to drop; and as a prudent physician does not in a moment apply a perfect cure to a disease, or effect a complete restoration to health, but employs salutary medicines after he has given nature an opportunity of first opening the way to recovery, so too the man endowed with virtue behaves with respect to the employment of the word which is in accordance with the law of wisdom. But the number seven is the sacred and dominical number, according to which the Father of the universe, when he made the world, is said to have looked upon his work. And the contemplation of the world, and of all the things contained in it, is nothing else but philosophy, and that excellent and select portion of it which wisdom contains, comprehending within itself also a work still more necessary to be seen.

(42) What is the meaning of the expression, "The dove returned a second time to him about evening, having in her mouth a leaf and a thin branch of olive?" (Genesis 8:11). All these separate points are selected and approved signs-the returning, the returning about evening, the having an olive-leaf and a thin branch of that tree, and oil, and the having it in her mouth; but yet every one of these signs can be examined with a certainty beyond certainty, for the return is distinct from its previous return, for that one bore with it an announcement of nature being wholly corrupted and rebellious, and being wholly destroyed by the deluge, that is to say, by great ignorance and insolence; but this second return brings the news of the world beginning to repent, but to find repentance is not an easy task, but is a difficult and laborious business. And it is on this account that the dove arrived in the evening, having passed the whole day from morning to evening in its visitations; in word, indeed, examining places, but in fact investigating the different parts of nature itself by continual visitation, and seeing them all clearly from beginning to end, for the evening is the indication of the end. The third sign, again, is its bringing a leaf; but a leaf is a small part of a tree, still it does not exist without a tree. And the beginning of displaying repentance is somewhat corresponding to this, since the beginning of correction has some slight indications about it, which we may call a leaf, by which it appears to receive guardianship, but can easily be shaken off; so that the hope shall in that case not be great of attaining the desired improvement, which is typified by the leaf of no other tree but of the olive alone, and oil is the material of light. For wickedness, as I have said before, is profound darkness, but virtue is luminous brilliancy, and repentance is the beginning of light. But you must not yet suppose that the beginning of repentance is only visible in branches just germinating and beginning to look green, but that it exists too while they are still dry, and while the seminal principle is dry and quiescent. And it is on this account that the fifth sign is shown, that, namely, of the dove when it comes bearing a slender branch. And the sixth sign is that this slender branch was in its mouth, for the number six is the first perfect number, since virtue bears in its mouth, that is to say in its conversation, the seeds of wisdom and justice, or, in one word, of honesty of the soul; and not only bears this, but gives some portion of participation in it even to the foolish, by drawing up water for their souls, and irrigating them with the desire of repentance for their sins.

(43) Why is it said, "And Noah knew that the waters had ceased from off the earth?" (Genesis 8:11). The literal statement is plain, since if the leaf had been taken up from off the water it would have been wet and soaked, but now he says that it was dry and slender, as if it had become dry by being on the earth which was dried. But with reference to its inward meaning, the wise man takes it as a symbol of repentance, and wishes to check the calamities of excessive obstinacy by taking the leaf, since it was not yet green, but slender, for the reason which has been already mentioned. At the same time we may admire the Father on account of his exceeding kindness, for although corruption had prevailed over all the men who lived on the earth from the excess of their iniquities, still there remained some relics of antiquity and of that which was from the beginning, and a slight seed of previous virtues; by which it is intimated nevertheless that the memory of all the good deeds that have been done from the beginning is not wholly destroyed. On which account a certain prophet, the kinsman and friend of Moses, uttered an oracle of this kind, "If the omnipotent Lord had not left us a seed, we should have been like blind and barren People,"{3}{Isaiah 1:9.} able neither to know the truth nor to generate it. And the Chaldaeans in their native language call blindness and sterility Sodom and Gomorrah.

(44) Why, in the third place, after seven other days, did he again send forth the dove, which did not again return to him? (Genesis 8:12). According to the word, the dove made no more return to him; but what in fact is meant is virtue, which, however, is not an indication of alienation, since, as I have said before, she was not separated from him at that time, but sent forth like a sun-beam to pay a visit of examination to the natures of others, but then, not finding any one to listen to her precepts of correction, she returns, and properly comes to him alone. But this time she is no longer the possession of one single individual, but is rather a common good to all those who have been willing to receive the emanations of wisdom as if coming up from the earth, those persons, that is, who from the very beginning have laboured under a great thirst of perfect wisdom.

(45) Why in the six hundred and first year of the life of Noah, and on the first day of the first month, did the waters of the deluge cease from off the earth? (Genesis 8:13). The word first, according to the defect of time, is spoken of with reference either to the month or the man, and each interpretation has reason to support it; for if we are bound to maintain that the water began to abate in the first month, we are equally obliged to consider that the sacred historian intended also to speak of the seventh month, that is, of that month which is the second equinox, since the same month is both the first and the seventh; that is to say, the first as respects nature and virtue, and the seventh in point of time. Therefore in another place he says, {4}{Exodus 12:2.} "This month is unto you the beginning of months, the first among the months of the year;" calling that the first which is so in respect of nature and virtue, and which as to number is in time the seventh month, since the equinox has its appointed order in regular series, and in point of time is assigned the better season of the year. But if you take that word first to have reference to the man, then it will be used with more truth, and with strict propriety, for the just man was truly and properly the first, as in a vessel the captain is the first man, and in a state the prince. But he is first not only in virtue, but also in order, inasmuch as in the very circumstances of the regeneration of the second sowing of the human race he was the beginning and the first. Moreover, it is very admirably considered with reference to this passage, that the deluge took place during the life of the first man, and that again, when it abated, things returned to their former steadiness, since after the deluge took place he had to live by himself with his whole family, and after that evil was removed he alone was found upon the earth during the latter period of his life until the regeneration of mankind began. But it is not to no purpose that this testimony is given both of the preceding portion of his life, and also of the later period, for he alone burnt with a desire for that genuine life which is in accordance with virtue, while all the rest of the world were hastening on to death by reason of their fatal wickednesses. Therefore of necessity the evil ceased on the six hundred and first year of his life, since in truth the destruction came with reference to the sixth number, and safety was restored in unity since unity is more a generativeness of the soul, and is the best for giving life, wherefore also a deficiency of water in the sea takes place at the new moon, in order that the units may be preferred in dignity both among months and years, when God saves those things which are upon the earth; since the man who cultivates just habits is called by the Hebrews in their native language Noah, but by the Greeks he is named Dikaios; however, he is not exempted from the laws affecting the body. For although he is not subordinate to the power of others, but is a prince, yet still, because he is nevertheless devoted to death, as he is dead, the principle of that number six is connected with unity; since it was not in one year taken separately that the deluge ceased, but together with the number six (as contained in the number six hundred), which is connected with it according to corporeality and inequality; since the other being a long number is in the first place six (that is to say, six hundred); on which account it is said, in the six hundred and first year. But the just man is so in his generation, not in that which is general, nor again in that in which he is just by comparison with the general corruption, but according to some especial generation; for his generation bears with it a certain comparison. But that man also is deserving of praise whom God selected beyond all other generations as being considered worthy of life, placing a limit to that life, and to him as being about to be both the end and the beginning of each generation and of each age; the end of that which is corruptible, the beginning of that which is to follow. And truly it is much more proper to praise him who, bending upwards with his whole body, looked up by reason of his friendship with God.

(46) What is the meaning of the expression, "And Noah opened the roof of the ark?" (Genesis 8:13). The text stands in need of no explanation. But with reference to its meaning, because the ark is symbolically our body, we must consider that that is spoken of as the roof of our body, which covers it and for a long time preserves its strength; such is concupiscence, by which the body is preserved and made to last, in a moderate degree, that is, and in accordance with the law of nature; as also it is dissolved by pain. When therefore the intellect is attracted by a desire for heavenly things it wishes to spring upwards, and in that way it bursts asunder every appearance of concupiscence; so that that thing being as it were removed which threw a veil of shade over it and obscured it, it might be able to apply its senses to undisguised and incorporeal natures.

(47) Why is it that the earth was dried up in the seventh month, and on the twenty-seventh day? (Genesis 8:14). Do you not see that he here calls that month the seventh, which a little while before he styles the first? for the seventh, as far as related to time, is the same, as I have said before, as that which is the first in nature, being the beginning of the equinox. But it is with great propriety that the beginning of the deluge is fixed to the seventh month, and the twenty-seventh day of the month; and again, the end and cessation of the deluge is fixed to the same seventh month and the same day; for, both the deluge and the removal of life took place at the equinox; the principle of which we have indicated a little time ago; for the seventh month is found to be synonymous with months and days of this time, and then again, the twenty-seventh day occurs with the same meaning, when the ark rested on the mountains. This is the month which by nature is the seventh, but in point of time the first, which in fact is the month of the equinox. Therefore, at the equinoxes a power of selection is given for seven months and twenty-seven days; for the deluge took place in the seventh month, on which the vernal equinox takes place; so that it is in time the seventh, but in nature the first. And the cessation of the deluge and the display of mercy belong to the same measure, when the ark rested on the tops of the mountains; again in truth in the seventh month, but not the same month, but in that in which the autumnal equinox occurs; that is to say, the seventh by nature, but the first in point of time. But the most perfect cure, the fact of the evil being wholly dried up, is again fixed to the seventh month and the twenty-seventh day of the vernal season; in order that both the beginning and the end of the deluge might find its boundary at the same season; and that the middle season when human life is repaired, is fixed to the intermediate season. In the meantime that expression is more certainly to be observed, namely, that the whole year, by a strict computation of days, made the deluge equal to the exact time of the remedy; for it began in the six hundredth year of Noah's age, in the seventh month, and on the twenty-seventh day; so that the whole space of the intermediate time completed a perfect year, the beginning being placed at the vernal equinox, and the flood also ending equally at the same epoch of the vernal equinox. And in this manner, after all things on earth, things full of fruit, had undergone destruction, as I have said before, now that the persons who used the fruits were also destroyed, the earth being wholly relieved of all evil was again found full of seeds and fruit-bearing trees, according to the production of spring; for he thought it reasonable that, as the earth after it had suffered the deluge was in a similar condition when dried again to that in which it was before, so it should now show itself, and pay the debt which it owed to nature. Nor ought any one to wonder that in one day the earth when left to itself produced every thing by divine virtue, both seeds and trees, all complete, entirely and suddenly, with perfect and excellent herbs, and grain, and plants, and fruits; since in the creation of the world on one day of the six he finished and brought to perfection the whole generation of plants. But the present fruits were already perfect in themselves, and produced all kinds of fruits in a manner suitable and corresponding to the season of spring; for all things are possible to God, who scarcely requires time to effect any thing.

(48) Why was it that after the earth was dried, Noah did not depart out of the ark, before he had received a fresh command from God, for God said to Noah: "Go forth, thou, and thy wife, and thy sons, and thy sons' wives, together with all the rest of the living creatures?" (Genesis 8:16). Justice is commonly inspired with fear, as on the other hand injustice is rash and self-confident. But the proof of a fear of God is the not giving up more to, or guiding one's self more by one's own reason than by God. And above all other men it was natural for that man who had seen the whole earth suddenly become an immense sea, to suspect that it might be possible that the same misfortune would again return. Besides this, he also gave a thought to the corresponding consequence, namely, that as he had entered into the ark at the command of God, so it was fitting that he should also leave it at the command of the same being; for let no one believe that he can ever do any thing perfectly unless God himself guides him by his preventing precepts.

(49) Why, when they entered into the ark was the order as follows: first himself and his sons, and after them his wife and his sons' wives, but when they went forth the order was changed, for the sacred historian says, "Noah and his wife went forth, and after them his sons and his sons' wives?" (Genesis 8:18). By the literal statement the sacred writer gives an obscure intimation, in the order in which they entered, that the propagation of seed was taken away, but by the order of their egress he implies the continuance of the process of generation; since, while they are entering, the sons are mentioned together which their father, and the daughters in-law with their mother-in-law, but when they are going forth the wives are all mated again, the father being accompanied by his wife, and each of his sons also by his wife, since he chose to show by fact rather than by words everything which it is fitting for his friends to do. Moreover he had in express words, and not by any vague intimations, commanded the men, as they were about to enter into the ark, that they while there were to keep themselves from connection with women; but now that they were about to depart from it, he plainly intimates to them that offspring is to be begotten in accordance with nature, by the order in which he appoints their going forth; nor did he employ words only, in order to make his proclamation about the state of the ark, saying, "After a destruction of all things on earth, of such a character and of such extent, do not indulge in pleasures, for that is not decorous. It is sufficient, however, for you to have received your lives; but while you are actually in the ark, to ascend up into the marriage bed with your wives would be a proof of your being devoted to lasciviousness." And, indeed, it was natural for them, as being relations to those who were being destroyed, to be moved with compassion for the perishing human race, especially because they themselves also were still in doubt whether, from some quarter or other, calamity might not fall also upon themselves; and besides these considerations it was absurd, while those who were alive were perishing, for those in the ark to be contriving that others who did not exist should be born, being warm at an unreasonable time, and burning with an inopportune desire. But after the anger of God ceased, then he commanded those who had been delivered from the calamity, when they had again gone forth out of the ark in order, to apply themselves to the procreation of a succeeding generation, when he tells us, that the men did not go forth with the men, nor the women with the women, but the wives with their husbands. But with respect to the inner meaning of this fact, we must say this, that when the mind is about to wash off and cleanse away its sins, then it is fit for male to live with male, that is to say, for the intellect, the chief part of the man, to be as a father, united to each separate thought, as a father to his sons, without any admixture of the female race, which is in accordance with the outward sense; since it is a time of battle, in which it is necessary to keep the order of the cohort distinct, and to preserve it strictly in order, that the soldiers may not be mingled in confusion, and so, instead of gaining a victory over the enemy, be conquered themselves; but when the purification is completed, and when the soul is dried up from all ignorance, and when a complete deliverance from everything pernicious has taken place, then it becomes the man to collect his scattered forces together, not in order that masculine counsels may be rendered effeminate by softness, but that the female race, that is to say, the outward senses, may clothe themselves with the vigour of the male, attaining to masculine counsels, and from their receiving seed for the production of a generation; so that, from this time forth they may cherish, in all things, sentiments of wisdom, and honour, and justice, and courage, and, in one word, of virtue. But, besides this, it will be reasonable also to take notice, that when once a confusion, in the similitude of a deluge, has overwhelmed the intellect, and when the different senses, being perplexed by the affairs of this world, like so many bulwarks erected against them, begin to quarrel, it is utterly impossible that any one should be able, either to sow, or to conceive, or to generate any good thing. But when all the hostile attacks of various agitations and passions are checked, and when the ceaseless invasions of lawless counsels are repressed, then the soul produces virtue and excellent works, as the most fertile portion of the earth, when dried, produces fruits.

(50) Why did Noah build an altar without having been commanded to do so? (Genesis 8:20). The requital of gratitude which is due to God ought to be offered to him without command, and without any delay or hesitation, showing the mind to be free from vices; for it becomes that man, who has been endued with blessings by God, to offer him his thanks with a grateful and willing mind; but he who delays to do so, waiting for an express command, is ungrateful, being as it were compelled by necessity honour his benefactor.

(51) Why is he said to have built an altar to God, and not to the Lord? (Genesis 8:20). In passages of beneficence and regeneration, as at the creation of the world, the sacred writer only refers to the beneficent virtue of the Creator, by which he makes everything in its integrity, and he implies this by concealing the royal name of Lord, as one which bears with it supreme authority; therefore now also, since what he is describing is the beginning of the renewed generation of mankind, he borrows for his description the beneficent virtue, which bears the name of God; for he used the kingly attribute, which declares his imperial power, by which he is called Lord, when he was describing the punishment inflicted by the flood.

(52) What is the meaning of the statement, "He took of the cattle and of the flying animals, and he offered whole burnt offerings on the altar?" (Genesis 8:20). All this is said with reference to an inward meaning, both because he received everything from God as a favour and gift; and also because he took of the clean sorts of animals, and burnt those which were unpolluted and clean, as entire and pure first fruits; for they are proper victims for good men to offer, and are themselves entire, being full of integrity; and they may be classed as fruits, for fruit is the end, for the sake of which the plant exists. This indeed is the literal statement; but with respect to the inner meaning, the clean cattle and the clean birds are the outward senses and intellect of the wise man, with the thoughts which are received in his mind; all which things it is reasonable to offer in their integrity as entire and perfect fruit, in the way of a display of gratitude to the Father, and to offer them to him as an unpolluted and clean oblation of a victim.

(53) Why does he offer his sacrifice to the beneficent virtue of God, but the acceptance of it takes place by means of both the qualities of the Lord and God, for Moses says, "And the Lord God smelled a savour of sweetness?" (Genesis 8:20). He says this since, when unexpectedly, after all hope is gone, we are preserved from dangers which are coming over us, we then, looking solely at the beneficence of him who has preserved us, do, on account of our joy, display ingratitude, and prefer the benefits which we have received rather to the beneficent power than to the Lord. But the beneficent preserver himself, by means of both his attributes, looks down upon and honourably accepts grateful minds, that he may not appear to halt in rewarding them; but he declares that such a display of gratitude is pleasing to both attributes of the one God.{5}{or, "But the one God very much likes to act by means of both his attributes."Note to the Latin version.}

(54) What is the meaning of the words, "And the Lord God said, repenting him, I will not again proceed to curse the earth for the works of man, for the thoughts of the mind of man are toward, and are diligently and ceaselessly exercised in, wickedness from his youth up; therefore I will not now proceed to smite all living flesh as I have done at other times?" (Genesis 8:21). The reasons alleged appear to indicate a change of purpose, which is an affection not usual nor akin to the divine virtue; for the dispositions of mankind are variable and inconstant, so that all affairs among them are altogether uncertain; but with God nothing is uncertain, nothing incomprehensible, for he is a being of mighty and consistent determination; how then, when reasons of the same kind are present to him, because he was forsooth aware from the very beginning that the mind of man was deliberately inclined to wallow in wickedness from his youth on, could he have originally intended to destroy the human race by a flood; and yet afterwards say, that he did not intend to destroy it any more, when the same evils still exist in the mind? But we must think that every kind of expression of this sort is, by law, connected with learning and the utility of instruction rather than with the nature of truth, since there are, as it were, two kinds which occur in the whole course of the law; in the first place, as it is said, "Not as a man;" and in the second place, as it is said, "As a man," the one God is believed to instruct his son. That first expression relates to the actual truth; for, in real fact, God is not as a man, nor again, as the sun, nor as the heaven, nor as the world, which is perceptible by the outward senses, but as God, if it is justifiable to assert that also; since that most happy and blessed being will not endure similitude, or comparison, or enigmatical description; nay, rather he surpasses even blessedness and felicity itself, and whatever can be imagined as better than and preferable to them. But the second expression relates to instruction and direction, I mean the express words, "As a man," in order that it may be observed, that he is willing to impress us beings, born of the earth, lest perchance we should unceasingly incur his anger and his chastisement by our implacable hostility to him, without any peace; for it is sufficient for him to be roused and embittered against us once, and once to exact vengeance against sinners; but to inflict punishment over and over again for the same thing is the conduct of a savage and ferocious disposition: since, says he, "when I shall inflict deserved retribution, as is possible, on every one, I will cause a burning recollection of my design to be preserved." Therefore behold, the sacred historian has excellently expressed himself, saying, "That God observed in his mind," for his mind and disposition rejoice in a superior degree of constancy; but our wills are found to be inconsistent and vacillating, on which account we cannot be properly said to observe and think with our minds, since it is by the thoughts that the passage of the mind is allowed to take place, {6}{"if you connect the Armenian words in a different manner, the sense will be 'meditation is the purification of the course of the mind,' and this is perhaps better." But the human intellect is unable to be extended over everything, since it is incapable of penetrating all things in a perfect and suitable manner. But that expression, "I will not proceed any more to curse the earth," is used with great propriety, for it is not becoming to add more curses to what has already been done, because the evils that have been inflicted are already complete; because, although they are in some sense imperfect, inasmuch as the Father is kind and merciful, and most humane, still he is rather inclined to alleviate the evil than to add to men's misery. But that is as it were the same thing, according to a common proverb, to wash a brick, or to draw water properly, and wholly to eradicate wickedness, with all its deeply imprinted tokens from the mind of man; for if it is implanted in it at first, it does not exist accidentally, but is engraven deeply on it and clings to it. But since the mind is a potential and principal part of the soul, he introduces that word "diligently;" but that which has been weighed with diligence and care is exquisite thought, examined more certainly than certainty itself. But this diligence does not tend to any one evil, but as is plain, to mischief, and to all mischief; nor does it exist in a perfunctory manner; but man is devoted to it from his youth, not only in a manner, but from his very cradle, as if he were in some degree united to, and nourished, and bred up with sin. But yet God says, "I will not any more smite all flesh;" giving notice that he will not, at any future time, destroy every portion of mankind altogether, but only single individuals, in ever such great numbers, who perpetrate unspeakable wickednesses; for he does not leave wickedness unpunished, nor does he grant it liberty or impunity, but indulging his care for the human race on account of his original design, he of necessity fixes destruction as a punishment for sinners.

(55) What is the meaning of the expression, "Sowing-time and harvest, cold and heat, summer and spring, shall not cease day nor night?" (Genesis 8:22). If taken literally this expression signifies the continuation of the duration of the annual seasons, and that the earthly temperature adapted to animals and plants is not again to be destroyed; since indeed, if the weather is corrupted it would corrupt them likewise, and if it is preserved in its existing state it would preserve them also safe and sound; for it is according to the weather and temperature that all animals and plants are preserved safe and sound, without any infirmity, being accustomed, in some measure, to be produced separately, in an admirable way, and to grow up together. But nature is like a harmony, composed of opposite sounds, both flat and sharp; for thus, also, the world is compounded of opposite qualities, for when, in the first place, the mortal commixtures of cold and heat, of moisture and dryness, preserve their natural order, without any confusion, they are themselves a cause which prevents destruction from overwhelming everything upon the earth. But if we regard the inward sense of the passage, the seed time is the beginning and the harvest time is the end, and both the beginning and the end are concurrent causes of safety, for either thing alone is by itself imperfect, because the beginning requires an end, and the end has a natural inclination for the beginning; but cold and heat bring round winter and autumn; for the autumn is fiery, but only in such a degree as succeeding in its annual revolution to cool the fiery summer. And, symbolically, with reference to the mind, cold indicates fear, since it causes terror and trepidation; but heat indicates anger, because an angry disposition bears in itself a resemblance to flame and fire; for it is necessary that those things should always exist and always remain among created and corruptible beings; since summer and spring have been instituted for the production of fruits; spring for the perfection of the seeds, and summer for the perfecting of fruits and the buds of trees. These things indeed are discerned symbolically in addition to the inward sense of the words, producing a double fruit; what is necessary being computed in the season of spring, and what is superfluous in the summer. Therefore necessary food is for the most part for the body, being whatever is produced freely from seeds; as virtues are necessary for the soul. But as many fruits as come by way of excess from trees in summer, besides the advantage which they are to the body, do also bring corporeal goods to the mind, as external advantages: for these external advantages are subservient to the body, and the body is subservient to the mind, and the mind to God. But day and night are the measures of times and numbers; and time and number exist without interruption. Day indicates lucid wisdom, and night betokens obscure folly.

(56) Why was it that God, blessing Noah and his sons, said, "Increase, and multiply, and replenish the earth, and rule over it; and let your fear and the dread of you be upon all beasts, and upon flying fowls, and upon reptiles, and upon the fishes which I have placed under your hand?" (Genesis 9:1). This devotion of the inferior animals to man, God also at the beginning of the creation bestowed on the sixth day upon man, after he had created him in his own image; for the scripture saith, "And God made man; in the image of God created he him; male and female created he them. And God blessed them, and said, Be fruitful, and multiply, and replenish the earth; and be ye lords over it, and be ye rulers of the fishes, and of the flying fowls, and of every creeping thing that creepeth upon the earth." And did he not by these words evidently intimate that Noah, at the beginning of what we may call the second creation of mankind, was found equal in honour to that creature who in the first instance was made as to his form in the likeness of himself? Therefore he equally assigned both to the one and to the other the principality and power over all the creatures that live upon the earth. But do thou diligently take notice that he showed this man, who at the time of the deluge was the only just man and the king of all the creatures which live upon the earth, to be equal in honour, not to the identical man who was first created and formed out of the earth, but to that one who was made according to the likeness and form of the true incorporeal entity, to whom also he gives power, making him a king, not the very created man (or the man formed out of the earth), but him who is according to his form and similitude, that is to say, incorporeal. Wherefore also the creation of that man, who as to his form is incorporeal, was marked to have taken place on the sixth day, in accordance with the perfect number six; but the creation of that man who was created after the completion of the world and subsequent to the generation of all animals on the seventh day, because it is after that that the manly figure was fashioned out of clay. Therefore after the days of generation he says, "on the seventh day of the world;" for God had not yet rained upon the earth, and no man did exist who could cultivate the earth. And then he proceeds to say, "But God formed a man out of the clay of the earth, and breathed into his face the breath of life, and man became a living soul." Therefore how he can be made worthy of the same kingly power according to the image of the man thus formed, he, I mean, who is the beginning of the second creation of mankind, is indicated by the letter of the history that relates these events. But with reference to the inward sense of the passage we must give an explanation in the following manner. God wills that the souls of wise men should increase in the magnitude and multitude of the beauty of their virtues, and should fill the mind as if it were the earth with those beauties, leaving no portion empty and void so as to become occupied by folly. And he

wills also that they should rule over, and strike terror into, and inflict alarm upon all beasts; that is to say, he wills that all wickedness should be subdued by their will, since wickedness is of an untamed and savage nature. Also he willed that they should be lords over all flying fowls, which by reason of their lightness are raised on high, being armed with courage and empty pride, and which thus cause the greatest mischief, being scarcely controlled at all by fear. Moreover, he made them rulers over all creeping things, which are the symbols of destructive vices, for they creep through the whole soul, namely, concupiscence, desire, sadness, and cowardice, striking and goading; as also they are indicated by the fishes, which eagerly cultivate a moist and delicate life, but one which is far from being sober, wise, or lasting.
(57) Why does God say, "Every creeping thing which lives shall be to you for food?" (Genesis 9:3). Creeping things are of a twofold nature; some being venomous, and others domestic. The venomous ones are serpents, which, instead of feet, use their bellies and breasts, creeping upon the earth; but the domestic ones are those which have legs above their feet. This is the literal meaning of the statement. But if we look to the inward sense of it, then the creeping things represent the foul vices, but the clean ones represent joy; for in connexion with the passion of concupiscence there will exist joy and pleasure; and in connexion with desire there will be will and counsel, and in connexion with sorrow goading and compunction, and in connexion with avidity there will be fear. Therefore such disordered perturbations of the passions threaten souls with death and destruction; but the joys do really live, as he himself has warned us in an allegory; and they also give life to those who possess them.
(58) What is the meaning of the expression, "As the green herb I have given you all things?" (Genesis 9:3). Some persons say that by this expression, "As the green herb I have given you all things," the eating of flesh was permitted. But I say that even though God had intended to give that permission, still that before all things he must have intended to establish by law the necessary use of herbs, that is to say of vegetables. And under the general name of herb he includes all the other additional descriptions of green food, without mentioning them expressly in the law. But now the power of this command is adapted not to one nation alone among all the select nations of the earth which are desirous of wisdom, among which religious continence is honoured, but to all mankind, who cannot possibly be universally prohibited from eating flesh. Nevertheless, perhaps the present expression has no reference to eating food, but rather to the possession of the power to do so; for in fact every herb is not necessarily good to eat, nor again is it the uniform and invariable food of all uniform living animals; since God said that some herbs were poisonous and deadly, and yet they are included in the number all. Perhaps therefore, I say, he means to express this, that all brute beasts are subjected to the power of man, as we sow herbs and take care of them by the cultivation of the land.
(59) What is the meaning of the expression, "You shall not eat flesh in the blood

of its life?" (Genesis 9:4). God appears by this command to indicate that the blood is the substance of the soul; I mean of that soul which exists by the external senses and by vitality, not of that which is spoken of with a certain especial pre-eminence, being the rational and intellectual soul; for there are three parts of the human soul; one the nutritive part, another that which is connected with the external senses, and the third that which exists in reason. Therefore the rational part is the substance of the divine spirit according to the sacred writer Moses: for in his account of the creation of the world, he says, "God breathed into his face the breath of life," as being what was to constitute his life. But of that part of the soul which is connected with the external senses and with vitality, blood is the substance; for he says in another place, "The blood exists in every breath of flesh." It is with great propriety in fact that he has called the blood the breath of all flesh, because there are in the flesh senses and passions, but not intellect nor thoughts. But again by the expression "the spirit of blood," he intimates that the spirit is one thing and the blood another; so that the essence of the soul is truly and beyond all possible question spirit. But that spirit has a place not by itself separately, apart from the blood in the body; but it is interwoven and mingled with the blood. As also the veins which exhibit a pulse, as if they were vessels to convey breathing, bear with them most unmixed and pure air, but blood likewise, though perhaps in a less degree; for there are two vessels, the veins and the breathing channels; but the veins have more blood than breath, and the breathing channels have more breath than blood. Therefore the proper admixture in each vessel is distinct, as the greater and the lesser proportion. This is the meaning of these words when taken literally; but if we look to their inner meaning, he calls the blood of the soul that warm and fiery virtue belonging to it which we name courage. And he who is full of this wisdom despises all food, and every pleasure of the belly, and of those parts which are below the belly. But if any one adopts a profligate life, and becomes a wanderer like the wind, and gradually inactive from laziness and a luxurious life, he in fact does nothing else but fall upon his belly, as a reptile creeping upon the earth, and greedily licking up earthly things, closing his life without ever tasting of that heavenly food which the souls which are desirous of wisdom receive.

(60) What is the meaning of the expression, "The blood of your souls will I require from every beast, and from the hand of man's brother will I require the life of man?" (Genesis 9:5). The multitude of creatures which do injury is twofold; some being beasts, and others men. But beasts are rather the least injurious of the two, because they have no actual familiarity with those whom they wish to injure, principally because they do not fall under their power, but destroy those who have properly power over them. But when he speaks of brothers, he means men who are murderers, intimating these three things. First of all, that all we men are akin to one another, and are brothers, being connected with one another according to the relation of the highest kind of kindred; for we have received a lot, as being the children of one and the same mother, rational nature. In the second place, he intimates that very commonly numerous and terrible quarrels arise, and acts of treachery take place, between relations, and rather between brothers, on account of the division of their inheritance, or on account of some superiority of dignity in the household; since a quarrel between those of the same family is worse and altogether unseemly, because brothers who are really so by the ties of nature meet in contest with a great knowledge of one another's internal circumstances; being therefore well aware what kind of attack they must employ in their present warfare. But, in the third place, as it appears to me, he employs the appellation of brothers in order to warn men of the implacable and severe punishment which is reserved for murderers; that they, without meeting any compassion, shall suffer what they have inflicted; for they have not slain strangers, but their own brothers in blood. It is with exceeding great propriety that he calls God the protector and overseer of those who are slain by man; for although men despise the revenge, yet let them not behave negligently, but although impure men of savage disposition escape for the moment from danger, still let them know that they are already caught and brought before the greater tribunal of justice, namely, before the divine judgment-seat, which rises up to inflict vengeance on the wicked for the defence of those who have received shameful and unworthy treatment. This is the literal meaning of the words; but if we look to the inward sense of them they have a regard to the merit of the purity of the soul, to which it is suitable to avoid unceasing destruction brought in from outward parts; which merit, that propitious and beneficent being, the most merciful and only Saviour, does not despise; but he expels and destroys all its enemies who stand around it, calling them beasts, and men brothers; for beasts are a symbolical expression for furious men threatening calamitous death; but men and brothers are both separate individual thoughts, and words uttered by mouth and tongue, because they are akin to them, and, by consequence, they bring on great and destructive evils, leaving no stone unturned, no work or word omitted to do injury.

(61) What is the meaning of the expression, "Whoso sheddeth man's blood by man shall his blood be shed?" (Genesis 9:6). There is no excess in this declaration, but rather an indication of a still more formidable denunciation, because he says, "He himself shall be poured out like blood who pours out blood." For that which is poured out flows forth and is lost, so that it has no longer any power or substance. And by this he shadows forth the fact that the souls of those who perpetrate unworthy actions imitate the mortal body in its corruption, as far as corruption is accustomed to come upon individuals; for the body is then dissolved into those parts of which it was composed, returning into its proper elements. But the miserable soul, labouring under distresses, is borne hither and thither by the overflow of a lascivious life; and the very evils which have grown up along with it are accustomed to suffer the same overflow, in the manner of the parts of the limbs.

(62) Why is it that he speaks as if of some other god, saying that he made man after the image of God, and not that he made him after his own image? (Genesis 9:6). Very appropriately and without any falsehood was this oracular sentence uttered by God, for no mortal thing could have been formed on the similitude of the supreme Father of the universe, but only after the pattern of the second deity, who is the Word of the supreme Being; since it is fitting that the rational soul of man should bear it the type of the divine Word; since in his first Word God is superior to the most rational possible nature. But he who is superior to the Word holds his rank in a better and most singular pre-eminence, and how could the creature possibly exhibit a likeness of him in himself? Nevertheless he also wished to intimate this fact, that God does rightly and correctly require vengeance, in order to the defence of virtuous and consistent men, because such bear in themselves a familiar acquaintance with his Word, of which the human mind is the similitude and form.

(63) What is the meaning of the words, "There shall not again be a deluge to destroy all the earth?" (Genesis 9:11). By his last saying he declares sufficiently that there may be various inundations, but that there shall never be one of such a character as to be able to change the whole earth into a lake or sea. This is the literal meaning of this saying. But if we look to its inward sense, there a divine kindness is intimated, according to which, although it is not every part of the soul which is allowed to make proficiency in every virtue, still some are adorned in a considerable degree. So that, supposing any one is not able to display excellence in his whole body, he still may labour with all diligence to acquire all the means in his power to display excellence; and that exertion is within his reach. And it does not follow that if any one is less highly endowed, or is unable to make every portion of his life altogether perfect, that he is on that account to despair of those things which he is able to do and to attain to. Since as there is power in every individual, he who does not exert himself in accordance with it is both idle and ungrateful; idle because of his laziness, and ungrateful because, though he has received most excellent means, he still sets himself in opposition to the essential qualities of things.

(64) Why does God say that, as a sign that he will never again bring a deluge over the whole earth, he will place his bow in the clouds? (Genesis 9:13). Some persons imagine that by the bow he means that thing which by some is called Jupiter's belt, from its figure, dwelling on its continual similitude to the rainbow; but I do not perceive that that has been positively asserted. In the first place, because the bow aforesaid ought to have a peculiar and essential nature of its own, because it is called the bow of God; for he says, "I will set my bow in the clouds." But that which belongs to God and is said to have been set in any place as his, indicates plainly that it is not devoid of essence or of substance. But the belt of Jupiter has not, properly speaking, any separate nature of its own, but is merely an appearance of the solar rays on a wet cloud, all the phaenomena of which are non-existent and incorporeal. And moreover, this is a further proof of that, that it is never seen at night, though clouds exist by night as well as by day. In the second place, we must also say that even in the day-time, when clouds obscure the whole face of heaven, the belt of Jupiter is never at all seen in them. But what remains may also be affirmed without any falsehood, when the Maker of the law says, "I will set my bow in the clouds;" for, behold, while clouds are present there is no appearance of the belt of Jupiter visible. But he said, "Where there is a collection of clouds let there be a bow seen in the clouds." Still it often happens, when the clouds are collected and when the air is obscured and thickened, that no appearance of a rainbow is seen anywhere. We must consider, therefore, whether haply the sacred historian indicates something else by this mention of the bow, namely, that in the very exercise of the mercy of God, and also in the moment of his bitterness towards men on earth, there still shall not be any ultimate destruction of them, in the fashion of a bow, which is too soft and unfit for such a purpose, nor shall there be any violence added, so as to cause a rapid destruction, but there shall be a moderate determination, each attribute being carefully measured; for the great deluge took place with a breaking asunder and disruption of the clouds and of all things; as he himself asserts, when he says, "The fountains of the deep were broken up." And yet it was not an unmeasured vehemence. Moreover, a bow is not itself a weapon, but only an instrument for the use of weapons, namely, for the arrow which strikes; and the arrow being sent forth by means of the bow strikes a part which is at a distance, while the parts which are nearest to it remain unhurt. And this is given as a proof that the whole earth shall never for the future suffer any deluge, since no one arrow ever hits all places, but only those which are at a distance. Therefore the divine virtue, being invisible, is symbolically indicated by the bow in the cloud; being in truth dissolved according to the figure of tranquillity, and condensed in accordance with a cloud; so that it does not permit all the clouds to be altogether dissolved into water, so that the earth may not be made a lake by an inundation, which it carefully forbids, and arranges the condensation of air, checking it as by a bridle, though it is at that time the more accustomed to exhibit itself as rebellious by reason of its excessive fulness. For by reason of the clouds it also shows itself to be replenished, dripping, and saturated.

(65) Why is it that after the sons of the just man have been named Shem, Ham, and Japhet, he relates only the generations of the middle one, saying, "And Ham was the Father of Canaan;" and afterwards he adds, "These are the three sons of Noah?" (Genesis 9:18). Mentioning four men, Noah and his sons, he says that these were obedient. Because the grandson Canaan was in his habits like his Father who begat him, on that account, instead of mentioning only one, he includes both in his enumeration, so that they are four in number, three in virtue. But in the meantime in the scripture he mentions only the generations of the middle one, on account of the just man whom he is going to speak of subsequently, because although he was his father, since Ham is the Father of Canaan, still he does not mention the father with blame, but with respect to the man with whom he thought it fair that the son should be a partaker, he yet did not give the father a participation with him. In the second place, perhaps he thus gives a premonitory warning also to those persons who by the acuteness of their mental vision can see a long way off what is at a distance, namely, that he designs to take away the land of the Canaanites from them after the lapse of many ages, and to give it to his chosen people who are thoroughly devoted to God. Therefore he chooses to designate the chief inhabitant of that region, namely Canaan, and to show that he both practised singular and peculiar wickedness of his own, and also all the wickedness of his father, so that in every part he might be convicted of an ignoble slavery and submission. This is the literal meaning of these words. But if we have a regard to the inward sense, he does not say that Ham had a son named Canaan, but he predicates offspring of him alone, saying, "Ham was the Father of Canaan." Since such a disposition as that of Ham is always the Father of such designs as those of Canaan, and that the very names themselves intimate this. For if we translate them into another language, Ham means heat or hot; and Canaan means merchants, or buyers, or causes, or recipients. Accordingly, he is not now speaking manifestly of generations, nor is he saying that one man is the Father or the son of another man, but he is evidently demonstrating the connection between one counsel and another, by reason of its alienation from all familiarity with virtue.

About the cultivation of the earth
(66) What is the meaning of the statement, "Noah began to be a cultivator of the earth?" (Genesis 9:20). He is here comparing Noah to the first created man who was formed out of the earth; for in that manner also does he speak of him when he came forth out of the ark; since both then and now there took place a first beginning of the cultivation of the land, each being after a deluge. For also, at the time of the original creation of the world the earth was, as it were, a lake, being covered by an inundation of water, for the sacred historian could not tell us that God said, "Let the waters be gathered together into one body, and let the dry land appear," unless it had previously been inundated with waters which now returned into certain depths of the earth. Nor again is the expression a purposeless one, "He began to be a tiller of the earth," for in the second generation he was himself the beginning of men, and also of seed, and of the cultivation of the land, and of the life of all other things. This is the literal meaning of the words. But if we look to their inner sense, a distinction is made between being a cultivator of the earth and a tiller of it; as the murderer of his brother is represented as tilling the earth, but not as cultivating it. For by the earth our body is symbolically represented, which is by its nature earthly, and which the unjust and wicked man tills like a lazy hireling, but which the man endued with virtue cultivates like a skilful manager of plants and an

agriculturist of good works appointed to superintend it. Because the workman of the body, the mind, as being carnal, procures carnal pleasures; but the cultivator of the earth is careful to produce useful fruits, those, namely, which are to be obtained by the study of continence, and modesty, and sound wisdom; and he prunes away all superfluous excesses and bad habits which spring up around, like the thin and misplaced branches of trees.
(67) Why does the just man first plant a vineyard? (Genesis 9:20). It was very natural for it to be a subject of anxiety and doubt to him in what quarter he was to find any plants after the deluge, when everything upon the earth was destroyed. Therefore it appeared natural, as was said a little while ago, that the earth was made dry in the spring season; therefore when the spring produced the buds of trees, the roots and stems of the vine could easily be found by the just man still alive, and might thus be collected by him. But we have to consider why the first thing he did was to plant a vineyard, and why he did not rather sow wheat and barley, since the latter are necessary productions of the earth, without which life cannot be supported, but the former is only a material for superfluous pleasure. The answer is that Noah, adopting a salutary design, consecrated and offered up to God those things which are necessary to support life and which require no co-operation for the production of the fruit; but the superfluous plants he devoted to men; for the use of wine is superfluous and not necessary. As therefore God ordered fountains of water fit to drink to burst up from the earth without the cooperation of man, so he also of his own accord granted to man in a similar manner wheat and barley, in order that he himself might be the sole giver of each kind of food which serves for necessary eating and drinking. But he did not take away the power nor grudge them providing for themselves by their own industry those things which contribute to pleasure.
(68) What is the meaning of the statement, "He drank of the wine and was drunken?" (Genesis 9:21). In the first place, the just man did not drink the wine, but a portion of the wine, not the whole of it; in which case an incontinent and debauched man does not quit his means of debauchery, till he has first swallowed all the wine that there is before him; but by the religious and sober man everything necessary for food is used in a moderate degree. And the expression, "he was drunken," is here to be taken simply as equivalent to "he used the wine." But there are two modes of getting drunk, the one is that of an intemperate sottishness which misuses wine, and this offence is peculiar to the depraved and wicked man; the other is the use of wine, and this belongs to the wise. It is therefore in the second of these meanings that the consistent and wise Noah is here called drunken, not as having misused but as having used wine.
(69) What is the meaning of the statement, "He was naked in his house?" (Genesis 9:21). This is a praise of the wise man both in the literal sense of the words, and also in their hidden meaning, that his exhibition of nakedness took place not out of doors but in his house, being concealed by the roof and walls of his house; for the nakedness of the body is concealed by a house which is made

of stones and beams of wood: but the covering and clothing of the soul is the discipline of wisdom. Therefore there are two kinds of nakedness, one which takes place by accident, which is the result of an involuntary offence, because the just man, using, if I may say so, his honesty as if it were a garment with which he is clothed, stumbles out of his own accord like men who are intoxicated, or who are afflicted with insanity; for in such men their offences are not deliberately committed: but it is his task and pleasing duty to clothe himself, as with a garment, with the discipline and study of honesty. There is also another kind of nakedness of the soul which is caused by perfect virtue, which expels from itself the whole carnal weight of the body, as if it were flying from a tomb, as indeed it has long been buried in it as in a tomb; as also it avoids pleasures, and also a great number of miseries arising from the different passions and many anxieties arising from misfortunes, and indeed all the evil effects of these different circumstances. He therefore, who has been able with distinction to pass through such various and great dangers, and to escape such injuries, and to emancipate himself from such evils, has attained to the destiny of happiness, without any stain or disgrace; for I should pronounce this to be the ornament and badge of beauty in those individuals who have been rendered worthy to pass their existence in an incorporeal manner.

(70) Why is it that the sacred writer has not simply said, Ham saw his nakedness, but Ham the father of Canaan saw the nakedness of his father? (Genesis 9:22). By stating the fact thus, he both blames the son in the father and the father in the son, as performing together in common the deed of folly, and iniquity, and impiety, and every other kind of wickedness. This is the literal meaning of the statement; and as to the inner sense, we must look at that in the same manner in which we have hitherto treated these subjects.

(71) What is the meaning of the statement, "He told it to his two brothers out of doors?" (Genesis 9:22). The sacred historian is here adding to the gravity of the transaction. In the first place, because he did not report the involuntary evil of his father to one brother only, but to both of them; and no doubt if he had had any more he would have told it to them all, as he did in fact to every one he could; and he did so with ridicule in his very words, making a jest of what ought not to have been treated with laughter and derision, but rather with shame and fear mingled with reverence. In the second place, when the historian says he told it them, not in the house but out of the house, he evidently points out that he displayed his father when naked, not only to his brothers, but also to the bystanders with whom they were, both men and women. This is the literal information conveyed by the words. But if we look to their inward meaning, then we shall see that a depraved and malignant habit of life is full of derision and contempt: and it is a bad thing to judge of the miseries of others even by one's self like a chastising judge. But in this case what has happened is worse than this, for any man with a joyful mind to ridicule the involuntary misfortune of a devoted disciple of wisdom, and to make a song of and proclaim abroad his misery, is the part of a thoroughly hostile accuser, who ought rather to have pardoned such an occurrence than to have added accusation or vituperation to it. Moreover, because these three things are, as I have said before, as it were brothers together; namely, good, bad, and indifferent, being all the offspring of one parent thought: in accordance with each of these principles, they have been found to be overseers, some celebrating virtues with praise, others upholding acts of malignity, and others supporting riches and honours and other good things which, however, are not attached to and which are external to the body. The overseers who emulate wickedness rejoice at the fall of the wise man, and ridicule and disparage him, as if he had done no good by the part which he adopts and to which he applies himself as better for the mind, or for his body, or for his external circumstances, to his internal virtues or to any of the good things which are around and exterior to his body. Unless indeed that man alone is eminently able to attain his object, who applies himself to iniquity, as that alone is accustomed to confer advantages on human life. Pronouncing these and similar precepts, those who are overseers of iniquity ridicule those who devote themselves to virtue, and to those things by which virtue is produced and consolidated: as some look upon those things to be which are around the body, and outside it, and which may be regarded in the light of instruments serving to that end.

(72) What is the meaning of the statement, "Shem and Japhet, taking a garment, laid it upon both their shoulders and went backwards, and covered the nakedness of their father, and they themselves did not see it?" (Genesis 9:23). The literal meaning of the statement is evident; but with respect to the inner sense contained in it, we must say that the light man who is in too great haste only sees those things which are before his eyes and exposed to his sight: but that the evil man also sees those things which are at his back, that is to say, the future. And since what is posterior is postponed to what is anterior, so is what is future to what is present, the sight of which is peculiar to the virtuous and wise man, who in truth is a second Lynceus, being according to the fables gifted with eyes in every part. Therefore every wise man, who is not so much man as actual intellect, walks backward, that is to say, he sees what is behind him or future, as if it were placed in brilliant light; and seeing every thing on all sides of him with a perfect sight, and looking all around him, he is found to be armed, and protected, and fortified, so that no part of his soul is ever found naked or in an unseemly plight, on account of any accidents which occur unfortunately.

(73) What is the meaning of the statement, "And Noah became sober after the wine?" (Genesis 9:24). The literal meaning is too notorious. Therefore we need only here speak of what concerns the inner sense of the words. When the intellect is strengthened, it is able by its soberness to discern with a certain accuracy all things, both before and behind it, both present, I mean, and future;

but the man who can see neither what is present nor what is future with accuracy, is afflicted by blindness; but he who sees the present, but who cannot also foresee the future, and is not at all cautious, such a man is overcome by drunkenness and intoxication; and he, lastly, who is found to be able to look all around him, and to see, and discern, and comprehend the different natures of things, both present and future, the watchfulness of sobriety is in that man.
(74) Why is it that after the sacred historian has enumerated Ham in the middle of the offspring of Noah, or has placed him in the middle between his brethren, he nevertheless points out that he was the younger, saying, "Noah saw what his younger son had done to him?" (Genesis 9:25). This is a manifest allegory, because he here takes as the younger, not him who was so in age and in point of time, but him who was younger in mind; since wickedness is unable to attain to a perception of the learning which is proper to the elder; but the elder thoughts belong to a will which is truly growing old, not indeed in body, but in mind.
(75) Why did Noah when praying for Shem speak thus: "Blessed is the Lord God, the God of Shem: and Canaan shall be his servant?" (Genesis 9:23). The names Lord and God are here used together on account of his principal attributes, both of benevolence and of kingly power by which the world was created; for as king he created the world according to his beneficence; but after he had completed it then the world was arranged and set in order by his attribute of kingly power. Therefore he at that time rendered the wise man worthy of a common honour, which the whole world also received, all the parts of the world being formed in an admirable manner with the attributes of the Lord and God, doing so by his especial prerogative, munificently pouring forth the favour and liberality of his beneficent power. And it is on this account that the beneficent power of God is mentioned twice. Once, as has been already stated, being placed in opposition to his kingly power; and a second time without any such connexion, in order, forsooth, that the wise man having been rendered worthy of his gifts, both such as are common to him with others and such as are peculiar to himself, he might also be rendered acceptable both to the world and to God; to the world on account of the excellence imparted to him in common with it, and to God for such as was peculiar to himself.
(76) Why, when Noah prayed for Japhet, did he say, "God shall enlarge Japhet, and bid him to dwell in the house of Shem: and Canaan shall be their servant?" (Genesis 9:27). Without examining the literal statement, for the meaning of that is plain, we had better approach the inner sense contained in it, and examine that, in which the second and third blessings mentioned are capable of an enlarged and ample extension. As, for instance, good health, and a vigorous state of the outward senses, and beauty, and strength, and opulence, and nobleness of birth, and friends, and the power of a prince, and numbers of other things. And on this account he said, "God shall enlarge," etc. Because taken separately, the abundant possession of such numerous and great

blessings has of itself been injurious to many persons who have scarcely dwelt with justice, or wisdom, or any other virtues, the complete possession of which dispenses to man in an admirable manner the advantages which are external to and which surround the body; but the deprivation or absence of them leaves him without the enjoyment or use of them; and man, if deprived of all good protectors, and of the use of these enjoyments, is exposed to as much suffering as he is capable of. Therefore he prays on behalf of he man who has those things which are around and exterior to the body, that he may dwell in the house of the wise man; so that attending to the rules of all good men he may see and regulate his own course by their example.

(77) Why because Ham had sinned did God pronounce that his son Canaan should be the servant of Ham and Japhet? (Genesis 9:27). In the first place, God pronounced this sentence because both father and son had displayed the same wickedness, being both united together and not separated, and both indulging in the same disposition. But in the second place, he did so because the father would be exceedingly afflicted at the curse thus laid upon the son, being sufficiently conscious that he was punished not so much for his own sake as for that of his father. And so the leader and master of the two suffered the punishment of his wicked counsels, and words, and actions. This is the literal meaning of the statement. But if we look to its inward meaning, then in reality they are no more two different men than two different dispositions. And this is made plain by the names given to them, which manifestly denote the nature of the facts; for Ham being interpreted means heat or hot; and Canaan means merchants of causes.

(78) Why was it that Noah lived after the deluge three hundred and fifty years? (#Ge 9:28). It is now declared that in two periods of seven years the form of the world was originally created and now renewed under Noah. But the wise man lives for a period of fourteen quarters of a century; and fourteen times twenty-five is equal to seven times fifty, or fifty times seven. And it is the principle of the seventh year and also of the fiftieth, which has an especial order of its own explained and ordained in Leviticus.

(79) Why among the three sons of Noah does Ham appear always to occupy the middle place, but the two extremities are varied; for when their birth is mentioned, Shem is placed in the first rank, in this manner, Shem, Ham, and Japhet; but when they are spoken of as fathers, then Japhet is mentioned first, and the beginning of the enumeration of the nations is derived from Japhet himself? (Genesis 10:1). Those who inquire into the literal nature of the divine writings think thus of the order in which these men are mentioned, looking upon him who is the first named, that is Shem, as the younger; and upon him who is named the last, that is Japhet, as the elder. However they may choose to think of this let them, being guided by the principle of mere opinion. But we who look to the real meaning of these statements think that there is here a reference to the three things, good, bad, and indifferent; which last are called secondary goods; and we must therefore think that the sacred writer always puts the bad in the middle, so that being confined at either extremity it may be subdued on one side by the one, and on the other side by the other; so that, being confined, it may be kept in and subdued. But the good and the indifferent, or secondary good, change the order with one another; for when there is such great evil present, and yet not wholly and altogether, the good rejoices in the first place, having the position of the dispenser and chief of the whole. But when it is placed in the position of the will in a state of conspiracy, and injustice remains not only in the intellect but is also conducted to its end by unjust works, then that first good is changed from its original order into another place, together with all the good habits which depend upon it, rejecting all education and all arrangement, as being wholly unable to attain its proposed end, just as a physician does when he sees an incurable disease. But the elder good manages that virtue which is around the body and exterior to it; therefore, by observing the extremities with greater caution, and closing in the beast within its toils, it is sufficiently demonstrated that it does not dare to bite or injure any more. But while it feels that it has done no injury, it is transferred into a more secure and more permanent position, and then, a higher and better fortified place being assigned to it, it easily retains the lower position too as one easy to be preserved; for, in consequence of the superior power of its guardian, it is always practicable to watch it closely, since nothing is more mighty than virtue.

(80) Why do the people of Ceos, and of Rhodes, and the isles of the Gentiles, spring from Japhet? (Genesis 16:4 - 5). Since he has the name denoting breadth (namely Japhet), being expanded in his growth and increase, that part of the things of the world which have been assigned by nature for the use of mankind, that is to say, the earth, can no longer hold him, therefore he passes over into the other part, that is to say, the sea and the islands belonging to it. This is the literal meaning of the statement. But if we look to its inner sense, all the external blessings which are bestowed by nature, such as riches, and honour, and principalities, are lavished and poured forth in every direction on those men into whose hands they come, and are also extended widely to others who are not so much within reach; so that in a greater, or at all events, in no less a degree do they surround and hem the man in, in accordance with the greediness of the lovers of riches and glory, since they are eager for principalities, and are never satisfied because of their insatiable desires.

(81) Why the eldest son of Ham is Chus. (Genesis 10:6). The sacred historian has here produced a word most completely in accordance with nature, saying that Chus was the elder son of evil, Chus being the dissolved and loose nature of the earth, for the earth, when dense and fertile, and moist, is full of herbs, and hills, and trees, and is well arranged for the production of different fruits; but when dissolved and reduced to dust and dry, it is unfruitful and barren; and besides it is tossed about in the air, when it is raised from the ground by the wind, by its dust making the air all alive. Such as this is the first origin and the first shoots of evil being destitute of the generation of good pursuits, and the cause of barrenness to the soul and to all its parts.

Why was Chus the father of Nimrod, who began to be a giant and a hunter before the Lord: on which account they said, "Like Nimrod the mighty hunter before the Lord?" (Genesis 10:8). The father in this case, having a nature truly dissolute, does not at all keep fast the spiritual bond of the soul, nor of nature, nor of consistency of manners, but rather like a giant born of the earth, prefers earthly to heavenly things, and thus appears to verify the ancient fable of the giants and Titans; for in truth he who is an emulator of earthly and corruptible things is always engaged in a conflict with heavenly and admirable natures, raising up earth as a bulwark against heaven; and those things which are below are adverse to those which are above. On which account there is much propriety in the expression, he was a giant against God, which thus declares the opposition of such beings to the deity; for a wicked man is nothing else than an enemy, contending against God: on which account it has become a proverb that every one who sins greatly ought to be referred to him as the original and chief of sinners, being spoken of "as a second Nimrod." Therefore his very name is an indication of his character, for it is interpreted Aethiopian, and his art is that of hunting, both of which things are detestable: an Aethiopian because unmitigated wickedness has no participation in light, but imitates night and darkness: and the practice of the huntsman is as much as possible at variance with rational nature, for he who lives among wild beasts wishes to live the life of a beast, and to be equal to the brutes in the vices of wickedness.

(1) What is the meaning of the expression, "I am the Lord thy God who brought thee out of the land of the Chaldaeans to give thee this land for an inheritance?" (Genesis 15:7). As the literal statement is plain enough, we need only consider the inner meaning, which was meant to be interpreted in this manner. The law of the Chaldaeans taken symbolically is mathematical speculation, one part of which is recognised to be astronomy, which the Chaldaeans study with great industry and with great success. Therefore God is here honouring the wise man with a gift; in the first place, by taking men out of the sect of the astrologers, that is to say, away from the hallucinations of the Chaldaeans, which, as they are difficult to detect and refute, are found to be the cause of great evils and wickedness, since they ascribe the attributes of the Creator to created things, and persuade men to worship and to venerate the works of the world as God. In the second place, God honours him by granting to him the wisdom which bears fruit, which he has here symbolically called the earth; but the Father of the universe shows that wisdom and virtue are invariable and immutable, since it is not consistent with his character that God should show to any one that which can undergo any variation or change, for that which is shown by the being who is immutable and consistent must be so too; but that which is liable to change, as being incessantly in the habit of suffering variation, admits of no proper or divine demonstration.

(2) Why does he say, "Lord, by what shall I know that I shall inherit it?" (Genesis 15:8). He here is seeking a sign for a ratification of the promise; but two things only are described deserving of study; one that which is an affection of the mind, namely, the belief in God according to his literal word; the other a being borne on with the most exceeding desire not to be left in want of some signs, by which the hearer may feel, to the conviction of his outer senses, a confirmation of the promise: and to him who has given the promise he offers worthy veneration by the appellation, "Lord." For by this title he says, I know thee to be the Lord and prince of all things, who art also able to do all things, and there is no disability with thee. But in truth, if I have already given credence to thy promise, still I nevertheless wish to obtain speedily if not a completion of it, yet at all events some evident signs by which its consummation may be indicated; in truth I am thy creature, and even if I were to arrive at the highest degree of excellence, I am not always able to restrain the violence of my desire, so as not, when I have seen or heard anything good, to be contented with obtaining it slowly and not immediately; therefore I entreat that thou wilt give me some means of knowledge, by which I may comprehend those future events.

(3) Why is it that he says, "Take for me a heifer of three years old, and a goat of three years old, and a raven of three years old, and a turtle dove and a pigeon?" (Genesis 15:9). He here mentions five animals, which are offered on the sacred altar; for these are divided into classes of victims, three kinds of terrestrial animals, the ox, the goat, and the sheep; and two kinds of birds, the turtle dove and the pigeon; for the sacred writer constantly tells us that the everlasting reverence of victims derived its origin from the patriarch, who was also the origin of the race: but instead of the expression, "Bring to me," he has very admirably used the words, "Take for me;" since there is nothing especially and peculiarly belonging to the creature, but everything is the gift of and blessing bestowed by God, who is altogether willing that when any one has received anything he should offer thanks for it with all his heart. But he orders him to take every animal at the age of three years; since three is a full and perfect number, consisting of a beginning, a middle, and an end; but still we may raise the question, why of these three animals, he takes two females, the heifer, and the she-goat, and one male, the ram; may it not be perhaps because the heifer and the she-goat are offered as an atonement for sin; but the sheep is not, as sin arises from frailty, and the female is frail? This much I have thought fit to say with especial appositeness to this question; but I am not however ignorant that all things of this kind offer a handle to those who wish to cavil, to disparage the sacred scriptures; therefore in this instance they say that there is nothing here described and indicated but a command to sacrifice, by the division of the animals and an examination of their entrails; and what is visible in them they affirm to be an indication of what is convenient, and of the similitude which arises from things visible. But those men, as it appears to me, are of that class which forms a part alone from a judgment of the whole, but which on the contrary does not from a judgment of a part from the whole, which last is the better way of coming to an opinion, as being that by which both the name and the fact are altogether established. Therefore the giving of the law, that is to say the sacred scriptures, that I may so express myself, is a sort of living unity, the whole of which one ought to examine carefully with all one's eyes, and so discern with truth, and certainty, and clearness, the universal intention of the whole of the scripture without dissecting or lacerating its harmony, or disuniting its unity; by any other mode everything would appear utterly inconsistent and absurd, being dissociated from all community or equity. What then is the intention of the delivery of the law as exhibited to us? It is scientific, and so is everything which describes scientific species; since the offering of sacrifice and all science admits of a consistent usage, and of expression well adapted to them, and of various opinions, by which not only the footsteps of truth are occupied, but sometimes are even darkened, as affection is by flattery; but in such way that the very things which are genuine and established by experiment are perverted by things which are both inconsistent and unproved. And the natures of the animals above mentioned have an intimate connection with the parts of the universe; the ox is connected with the earth, as being an animal employed in drawing the plough and in tilling the earth; the goat again is connected with the water (it is called in Greek and Armenian aix, or ajx), being an animal deriving its name from driving and rushing on (from ago ฅ or aisso ฅ); since water is an impetuous thing, and the course of rivers, and the extent of the breadth of the sea, and the sea itself agitated as it is by its ebb and flow, are witnesses of the propriety of the name and of the closeness of the connection. And the ram (aries) is connected with the air, as being a very violent and vivacious animal, on which account too the ram is more useful to mankind than any other animal as affording them raiment. Therefore, on account of these reasons, as I think, God orders him first to take these two female animals, the cow and the she-goat; since both these elements, earth and water, are material, and for the most part feminine. But the third he will have a male, namely the ram; because the air or wind has been explained as masculine; since the natures of all things are divided into bodies or into earth and water, and female animals exist by nature. But that which exhibits a similitude to the soul is arranged under the head of air and the breath of life. And this, as I have said, is masculine. If therefore we are to call that masculine which is the moving and active cause we must call that feminine which is moved and passive. But the whole heaven is found to be familiarly connected with flying birds such as the pigeon and turtle dove, being distributed as it is into the rotatory path of the planets and fixed stars. Therefore he dedicates the pigeon to the planets, for that is a tame and domestic animal, as also the planets are more familiarly connected with us as being nearer to the earth, and as having sympathies with us; but he consecrates the turtle dove to the fixed stars, for that animal is a lover of solitude, and flees from the conversation of the multitude, and from all connection of every kind. And so also the globe itself is remote, and a thing which wanders into the furthest extremities of the world. Therefore both the species of these two birds are assimilated to the divine attributes, since as Plato, the disciple of Socrates, says it is fitting that the heaven should have a swift chariot by reason of its very swift rotatory motion, which in fact surpasses even the birds themselves in the velocity of their course. But the birds above mentioned are singers; the prophet indicating by an enigmatical expression that perfect music which exists in heaven harmoniously adapted from the motion of the stars, since it is a proof of human art when the corresponding music of the voices of animals and of living instruments is adapted together by the industry of genius. But this heavenly music has been abundantly extended over the earth by the Creator, as he has also extended the rays of the sun, being always prompt to exercise his beneficent care for the human race. For such music excites frenzy in the ears, and brings unrestrained pleasure to the mind; and so causes men to forget even their meat and drink, and even when hunger brings death to the door to be willing even to die out of a desire to hear music. And if the song of the Sirens, next where the Sirens dwell, you plough the seas; / Their song is death, and makes destruction please. / Unblest the man, whom music wins to stay / Nigh the curst shore, and listen to the lay; / No more that wretch shall view the joys of life, / His blooming offspring, or his beauteous wife! / In verdant meads they sport, and wide around / Lie human bones that whiten all the ground; / The ground polluted floats with human gore, / And human carnage taints the dreadful shore." And further on in the same book, the poet describes the effect of these songs upon Ulysses, Od. 12.183c~194 o stay, O pride of Greece! Ulysses, stay! / O cease thy course and listen our to lay! / Blest is the man ordained our voice to hear, / The song instructs the soul, and charms the ear. / Approach! thy soul shall into raptures rise! / Approach! and learn new wisdom from the wise! / We know whate'er the kings of mighty name / Achieved at Ilion in the field of Fame; / Whate'er beneath the sun's bright journey lies. / O stay and learn new wisdom from the wise!" As Homer tells us, invites the heathen so forcibly, that they forget while listening to it, their country, their houses, their friends, and necessary food; how much more must that most perfect and consummate music, so truly heavenly and endowed with the highest degree of harmony, when it touches the organs of the ear, compel men to go mad and to yield to rapture. But the reason on account of which every one of the animals to be offered is to be three years of age has already been explained; and we must now discuss it under another form of mystery, since it has been seen that every one of those things which were called into existence and subsequently to the moon, such as the earth, water, and air, rejoice in an order connected with the number three. In the divisions of earth there is a vast quantity of dry continent, islands and peninsulas. Water is divided into sea, rivers, and lakes; and the air into the two equinoxes, the vernal and the autumnal; and they may be taken as one, for they have an equal proportion of day and night, and accordingly the equinoxes are neither hot nor cold. Add to these the changes of summer and winter, for the sun is borne through those three circles into the seasons of summer, winter, and the equinoxes. Therefore, in the first place, the natural arrangement will be of this kind; and the moral arrangement is properly thus. In every one of us there are three things: flesh, the outward sense, and reason; therefore the calf exhibits a familiarity with the corporeal substance, since our flesh is subdued by, and kept in subservience to, and in connection with the ministrations of life; also their nature is female according to matter, being calculated rather to be passive and to be subject rather than the be active. But the similitude of the she-goat is connected with the communion of the outward senses, either because all the objects of those outward senses are each borne towards their appropriate sensation, or because each impulse and motion of the soul takes place in consequence of an imagination formed of the objects received through the medium of the external senses. And this is followed, in the first place, by a certain inflexion or alienation, which by some is called an occasion, that is to say, an impulse affecting each kind of sense. But since the female is the outward sense, as being passive on consequence of what is subjected to the outward senses, therefore God has adapted to it a female animal, the she-goat. But the ram is akin to the word, or to reason. In the first place, because it is a male animal; secondly, because it is a working animal; and thirdly, because it is the cause of the world, and of the firmament; that is to say, the ram is so by means of the clothing which it supplies; and reason, or the word, is so in the arrangement of life; for whatever is not irregular and absurd immediately exhibits reason. And there are two species of reason; the one derived from that nature by which the affairs of the world subjected to the outward senses are finished; the other from that of those things which are called incorporeal species, by which the affairs of that world which is the object of the intellect are brought to their accomplishment. Therefore the pigeon and the turtle dove are found to resemble these. The pigeon, forsooth, resembles speculation in natural philosophy; for it is a more familiar bird, as the objects of the outward sense are exceedingly familiar to the sight: and the soul of the inquirer into natural science flies upward as if it were furnished with wings; and being borne aloft is carried round the heaven, discerning every part of every thing, and the principles of every separate thing; for the turtle dove imitates that species which is the subject of intellect and incorporeal; for as that animal is fond of solitude, so it is superior to the violent species which come under the outward sense, associating itself as it does with the invisible species by its essence.

(4) Why does he say, "And he took unto him all these things?" (Genesis 15:10). He has added also that expression, "And he took unto him," with especial propriety; for it is the sign of a soul thoroughly imbued with the love of God to ascribe whatever good and noble theories and feelings it receives, not unto itself, but wholly to God who is the giver of all benefits.

(5) What is the meaning of, "He divided them in the middle and laid the pieces opposite to one another?" (Genesis 15:10). Also the whole structure of the body, as of flesh, is to be looked at in such a light as this according to its whole creation; for the parts are brothers; not as they are divided and placed opposite to one another; but, being naturally inclined to one another, and having a mutual regard to one another, on account of their natural co-operation; the original Creator who gave them life making this division for the sake of usefulness, so that one part should be opposed to the other part, and again that both should reciprocally seek one another in all necessary ministrations. In this way he has directly separated the sense of sight, distributing it equally to two eyes by placing the nose between them and thus turning each eye to the other; for the pupils, if I may so say, lean both in one direction so as mutually to behold the same thing, scarcely ever straying beyond the position in which they are placed, but only looking towards one another, especially when anything comes across their sight. And in similar manner the faculty of hearing is distributed between the two ears, which are both reciprocally turned to one another, both tending to one and the same operation. And the sense of smell is divided between the two nostrils, being turned towards the two tubes of the nostrils, which are not revolving around or inclined towards the cheeks, so as being drawn in two different directions to look the one towards the right and the other towards the left, but being both collected together and turned inwards they await all smells with a common action. So also the hands are not made of an appearance contrary to that of one another, but being like brothers and like divisible parts, looking to one another mutually, and being prepared by nature for an operation and employment suitable to them, they thus act in the operations of receiving, giving, and working. And the feet are not constituted differently from the hands; as each of them behaves in such a manner that they both yield the one to the other, and progress is effected by the motion of both together, so that nothing can be accomplished by one alone. Nor is it only the feet and shins, but also the legs and knee-pans, and hips, and the breasts, and in fact every part on the right or left of the body, being divided in a similar manner, indicate one general harmony and correspondence and union as it were of connatural parts; that is to say, of all of those different members enumerated according to their separate species. And generally, whoever considers together and in an equal manner all the above mentioned parts thus subdivided, in reference to their joint operation, will find one nature combined of the two parts. As the hands, united and connected together with the fingers, are seen when in union with them to exhibit a harmony; and the feet, when re-united in operation, are seen to tend to union; and the ears, when similarly combined in the figure of an amphitheatre, are seen to unite themselves, in effect extending across the space which separates them. Therefore our nature, continually making in this manner a division of those parts which exist in us according to each separate species, has first of all separated and arranged the different sections, placing them as it were opposite to one another in the same way in which it has arranged the world; and it has also arranged them with reference to the easy discharge of their several duties. And again it has combined each of these members according to each species into one action, and into the same operation, collecting together all of them when considered generally. Nor is it only the parts of the body which any one may see thus united and in pairs, separated in their union, and again united in their division, but the parts of the soul are so too. But since the two superior sections of this are so many separate classes, namely the rational and the irrational, so also the separate parts of each section have their own appropriate division; as for instance, the rational part is divided into the intention and into the uttered word; and that part which exists in accordance with the outward senses is divided into the four senses; for the fifth sense, touch, is common to the other four, two of which, those with which we see and hear, are philosophical senses, so that it is by means of them that the power of living well is acquired for us; the others are nonphilosophical, namely smell and taste, but are servile, being created only for living; for the sense of smell, by means of its exercise, contains many things which awaken it, and receives a continual breathing which is as it were the continual food of living creatures; therefore smell and taste support this mortal body, but sight and hearing afford service to the immortal soul. Therefore these divisions of our members, according to our body and soul, were made and separated by the Creator; however, we must know that the parts of the world also are arranged in two divisions and are placed opposite to one another; the earth being divided into mountainous and champaign districts; the water into sweet and salt, sweet being that which is supplied by springs and rivers, and salt being that which comes from the sea; as also the atmosphere is divided into summer and winter, and also into spring and autumn. And it is on this account that Heraclitus wrote his books about nature, having borrowed his theory of contraries from our sacred historian, with the addition of an infinite number of laborious arguments.

(6) Why is it said, "But he did not divide the birds?" (Genesis 15:10). He is shadowing forth a fifth and periodical nature, from which the ancients say that the heaven was made; for the four elements are mixtures rather than elements: by which he subdivides those things which are already divided into those materials of which they were originally composed, as the earth includes within itself a portion of the elements of water, and also of air, and also of fire, which however obtains the appellation not so much in accordance with our apprehension of it, as with our sight; and again the water is not so clear or pure, as not to have some participation in wind and earth; and so also in each of the other elements there is a certain tempering and combination; but the fifth substance is the only one which has been made unmixed and pure, on which account it was not accustomed to be mentioned at all. Therefore it is well said, he did not divide the birds; since the heavenly nature, both of the planets and also of the fixed stars, is raised on high like that of birds, in the similitude of both kinds, that is to say, of clean birds, the turtle dove and the pigeon, which scarcely admit of being divided or cut up; for the indivisible nature is of a fifth essence, more unmixed and pure than the others, and therefore it more closely resembles unity.

(7) What is the meaning of, "And the birds descended on the bodies which were divided?" (Genesis 15:11). Since the three animals, the heifer, and the shegoat, and the ram, were divided in a symbolical manner, they are signs, as we have already said, of the earth, and water, and air; still it is necessary to give now a reason for this, examining the truth carefully under the mystery of a similitude. Perhaps therefore he designs and intimates by the descent of the birds on the cut pieces an invasion of enemies; for all the nature of the world beneath the moon is full of battles and ill will, both domestic and external; and the birds in truth appear to fly down on the divided bodies for the sake of meat and drink; naturally indeed it is the stronger which descend upon the weaker animals, as upon dead bodies, attacking them in general unexpectedly, but they do not fly down on the turtle dove and pigeon, since the heavenly bodies are free from desires and unconscious of suffering wrong.

(8) Why is it that he says, "Abraham passed over and sat upon them?" (Genesis 15:11). Those who think that sacrifice is indicated by the matters about which we are at present speaking will say that the virtuous man, sitting as it were in a synagogue, has examined into the entrails of the divided animals, as if that were looked upon as an unerring symbol for the declaration of the truth; but we, who adhere to Moses and who are thoroughly acquainted with the views of that teacher, one who, turning away his face from every sophistical appearance and prognostic, trusted in God alone, will rather say, that he has here introduced the just man who is endued with virtue with the birds themselves, who were congregated together and flying about over him, intending to denote nothing else by this parabolical presentation, but that he is desirous of hindering injustice and covetousness, and is most hostile to quarrels and wars, and a lover of consistency and peace; for he himself is truly a guardian of peace. Since no one state has ever rested in tranquillity owing to the conduct of the wicked, but kingdoms have become fixed steadily when one or two men endued with virtue have arisen, whose virtue has put an end to civil disturbances, God granting to those who are earnest in the pursuit of virtue good habits calculated to procure them honour; and not to them only, but to those also who approach near to the production of general advantage.

(9) What is the meaning of the words, "About the time of the setting of the sun a trance fell upon Abraham; and lo, a great horror of darkness came over him?" (Genesis 15:12). A certain divine excess was suddenly rendered calm to the man endued with virtue; for the trance, or ecstacy as the word itself evidently points out, is nothing else than a departure of the mind wandering beyond itself. But the class of prophets loves to be subject to such influences; for when it is divining, and when the intellect is inspired with divine things, it no longer exists in itself, since it receives the divine spirit within and permits it to dwell with itself; or rather, as he himself has expressed it, as spirit falls upon him; since it does not come slowly over him, but rushes down upon him suddenly. Moreover, that which he has added afterwards applies admirably, that a great horror of darkness fell upon him. For all these things are ecstacies of the mind; for he also who is in a state of alarm is not in himself; but darkness is a hindrance to his sight; and in proportion as the horror is greater, so also do his powers of seeing and understanding become more obscured. And this is not said without reason: but as an indication of the evident knowledge of prophecy by which oracles and laws are given from God.

(10) Why was it said to him, "Thou shalt know to a certainty that thy seed shall be a stranger in a land that is not theirs, and shall be reduced to slavery, and shall be grievously afflicted for four hundred years?" (Genesis 15:13). That expression is admirably used, "It was said to him," since a prophet is supposed to utter something, but yet he is not pronouncing any command of his own, but is only the interpreter of another who sends something into his mind; and moreover whatever he does utter and deliver in words is all true and divine. And in the first place, he declares that a family of the human race is to dwell in a land belonging to another; for all things which are beneath the heaven are the possession of God, and those living creatures which exist on the earth may

more properly and truly be said to be sojourners in a foreign land than to be dwelling in a country of their own which by nature they have not got. In the second place, he thus declares to us that every mortal is a slave after his kind. But no man is found to be free, but every one has many masters who vex and afflict him both within and without; for instance, without there are the winter which affects him with the cold, the summer which scorches him with heat, and hunger, and thirst, and many other calamities; and within there are pleasures and concupiscences, and sorrows, and fears. But his servitude is limited to a period of four hundred years, during which the aforesaid pleasures shall rise up against him. On which account it has been said above, that Abraham passed over and sat upon them, hindering and repelling them; as far as the literal words go, repelling those carnivorous birds which were hovering over the divided animals, but in fact repelling the afflictions which come upon men. Since a man who is in his own proper nature a lover of, and also by diligent practice a studier of virtue, is a most humane physician of our race, and a true protector of it, and guardian of it from evil. For all these things have an allegorical reference to the soul. For while the soul of the wise man, descending from above from the sky, comes down upon and enters a mortal and is sown in the field of the body, it is truly sojourning in a land which is not his own. Since the earthly nature of the body is wholly alien from pure intellect, and tends to subdue it and to drag it downwards into slavery, bringing every kind of affliction upon it, until the sorrow, bringing the attractive multitude of vices to judgment, condemns them; and thus at last the soul is restored to freedom. And it is on this account that he subsequently adds the sentence, "Nevertheless the nation which they shall send I will judge: and afterwards they shall go forth with great substance;" namely, with the same measure, and still better. Because then the mind is released from its mischievous colleague, departing out of the body and being transferred not only with freedom but also with much substance; so as to leave nothing good or useful behind to its enemies. Since every rational soul is productive, but he who thinks himself loaded and endued with virtue in his own counsel, is unable to preserve his fruit unto the end. For it becomes a virtuous man to attain to the objects which he has intended of his own accord, as also the counsels of wisdom correspond to those objects. Since, as some trees, although they appear productive at the first season of the budding of their fruits, are yet unable to bring them to maturity, so that the whole fruit before it becomes ripe is shaken off by every trifling cause; in the same manner the souls of inconstant men feel many influences which contribute to their productiveness, but nevertheless are unable to keep them sound till they arrive at perfection, as a man studious of virtue ought to do in order eventually to gather them as his own possessions.
(11) What is the meaning of, "But thou shalt go to thy fathers in peace, being nourished in a fair old age?" (Genesis 15:15). He here clearly indicates the incorruptibility of the soul: when it transfers itself out of the abode of the

mortal body and returns as it were to the metropolis of its native country, from which it originally emigrated into the body. Since to say to a dead man, "Thou shalt go to thy fathers," what else is this but to propose to him and set before him a second existence apart from the body as far as it is proper for the soul of the wise man to dwell by itself? But when he says this he does not mean by the fathers of Abraham his father, and his grandfather, and his great-grandfathers after the flesh, for they were not all deserving of praise so as to be by any possibility any honour to him who arrived at the succession of the same order, but he appears by this expression to be assigning to him for his fathers, according to the opinion of many commentators, all the elements into which the mortal man when deceased is resolved. But to me he appears to intend to indicate the incorporeal substances and inhabiters of the divine world, whom in other passages he is accustomed to call angels. Moreover the words which follow are not by any means without an object, that he is nourished in peace and in a fair old age. For the wicked and depraved man is nourished in battle, and lives and departs in a very bad old age. But the good man, in both phases of existence, both in that which is in connection with the body and in that which is apart from the body, cultivates peace, and is alone completely virtuous, such as no foolish person is found to be, even though he should live longer than an elephant; on which account he here carefully said, "Thou shalt go to thy fathers, being nourished-not in an advanced old age, but-in a fair old age." For many foolish persons also have their lives extended to a greatly lengthened period, but it is only the man who is desirous of virtue who enjoys a good old age and one endued with virtue.

(12) Why is it that he says, "And in the fourth generation they shall return again hither?" (Genesis 15:16). The number four is more fit than any other number, for this reason, that as it is more perfect, and is the root and foundation of the perfect number ten; and it is according to the principle of the number four that all collected are to return hither, as he himself has said. But as he by himself is perfect, so also those of whom he is the father are evidently perfect. But what is it that I am saying? In the generation of animals the sowing of the seed has the first place; in the second place, comes the fact of each instrument being, in some manner, impressed by something akin to nature; thirdly, there is the growth after the first formation of the creature; fourthly, after everything else comes the perfection, that is to say, the birth. And the same principle and order prevail in plants; the seed is cast into the earth, then it pushes its way both upwards and downwards, partly in roots and partly in branches; after that it increases; and fourthly, it produces fruit; and in the same manner again the trees, when made, first of all produce fruit, which subsequently grows; then, as it becomes ripe, it changes colour; and, fourthly, and this is the last operation, it completes and perfects its work, the consequence of which is the use and enjoyment of it by men.

(13) What is the meaning of, "For the sins of the Amorites were not as yet completed?" (Genesis 15:16). Some persons have said, that by this expression of the principle of Moses fate is expressly introduced, as if, in truth, everything was to be accomplished according to some particular hour and appointed period of time.

(14) What is the meaning of, "And when the sun was in the west a flame arose?" (Genesis 15:17). It means either that the sun himself appeared in the west in the similitude of a flame, or that some other flame appeared at eventide, not lightning, but some fire like it, which descended from above. The manifest interpretation of the oracle is this; but we must now discuss that which regards the inner sense.

(15) What is the meaning of the expression, "Behold there was a smoking furnace and torches of fires, which passed through the middle of those divisions?" (Genesis 15:18). The literal meaning of the statement is plain, for the fountain or root of the divine word will have the victims consumed, not by that fire which is given for our use, but by that which descends from above, out of heaven, in order that the purity of the essence of heaven may bear witness to the sanctity of the victims. But if we regard the inward meaning of the words, all things which are done beneath the moon are here compared to a smoking furnace, on account of the vapour which rises up out of the earth and water. As also the divisions of nature are, as has been already shown, every portion of the world being divided into two parts; and by these there are kindled, as it were, torches of fire, being powers which are more rapid in motion and more efficacious, being burning, in truth, like divine fiery discourses, at one time keeping the whole universe in a state of integrity reciprocally with themselves, and at another cleansing away the superfluous darkness. But the following interpretation may also be given with propriety in a more familiar manner. Human life is like unto a smoking furnace, because it has not a pure fire and an unalloyed brilliancy, but a great deal of smoke, smoking darkly through the flame, which causes mist and darkness, and an obscuration, not of the body but of the soul, so that this last cannot discern things clearly, until God the redeemer commands the heavenly lamps to arise, I mean those more pure and more holy radiations which unite those parts previously divided in two, on the right hand and on the left, and, at the same time, illuminate them, being the causes of harmony and of lucid clearness.

(16) Why did he say, "On that day, God made a covenant with Abraham, saying, To thy seed will I give this land, from the river of Egypt to the great river Euphrates?" (Genesis 15:19). The literal expression describes the boundaries of the space which lies in the middle, between the two rivers Egyptus and Euphrates, for anciently the river was also called by the same name as the district, Egypt, as the poet also testifies when he says: "And in the river Egypt did I fix my double-oared Ships." But if we look to the inner meaning of the expression, it intimates happiness, which is the perfect fulness of three good things, namely, of spiritual, and corporeal, and external blessings, as some of those men describe it in their panegyrics, who were afterwards called philosophers, such as Aristotle and the Peripatetics; nevertheless, such a giving of the law as this is called Pythagorean. Therefore the Egypt is a symbol of corporeal and external blessings, and the Euphrates of spiritual advantages, in which alone, it is plain, their real joy consists, which has wisdom and all the other virtues for its foundation; and the boundaries of this happiness are very rightly described as beginning with the Egyptus and ending with the Euphrates; for the things affecting the soul come at the end, which we usually approach with difficulty after we have passed through corporeal and external things, in such a manner that, by this progress, we have felt our unity, the integrity of our outward senses, and the beauty and strength which existed in our youth, advance, increase, and come to maturity. And in a similar manner, those things which relate to acquiring gain and to trafficking, as the management of ships, and agriculture, and commerce; for it is well said, that all things, especially those above-mentioned, become a young man.

(17) Who are the Kenites, the Kenezites, and the Kadmonites, and the Hittites, and the Perizzites, and the Rephaims, and the Amorites, the Canaanites, the Girgashites, and the Jebusites? (Genesis 15:20). Ten nations of wickedness are here enumerated, which he here destroys because of their neighbourhood, since the number ten, when false and improperly stamped, is very near to that which is good and an object of affection; but the complete perfection of the number ten is exceedingly fit, as being the measure of infinite numbers, since the world is arranged in accordance with it, and so likewise is the mind of the wise man, the substance of which, nevertheless, wickedness perverts and overthrows, despising all very necessary powers, so that that alone remains which the sacred writer has said, namely, that the pursuit of virtue is a blessing, for the wicked man is such that he embraces vague opinions rather than truth, and of such is Ishmael, though the seed of the prophets.

(18) Why it was that Sarah, the wife of Abraham, bore him no children? (Genesis 16:1). The mother of opinion is here spoken of as barren. In the first place in order that the son of generation might appear more wonderful, as being born by a miracle. In the second place in order that his conception and nativity might appear to be owing not more to the marriage of the man than to divine providence. For it is not owing to the faculty of conception that a barren woman should bear a son, but rather to the operation of divine power. This is the literal meaning of the statement. But if we look to its inward sense, then we shall say, in the first place, that to bring forth is peculiar to the female sex, as to beget is the office of the male: therefore God wills in the first place to render the mind, which is filled with virtue, like to the male sex rather than to the female, thinking it suited to its character to be active, not passive. In the second place both do generate, both the virtuous mind and the wicked one: but they generate in a different manner, and they produce contrary offspring, the virtuous mind producing good and useful things, but the depraved or wicked mind producing base and useless things. In the third place he who is still advancing and making progress is to be incited to the summit itself, and is near to the light which by some persons is said to be delivered to oblivion, and to be made unknown. He therefore, as he is making progress, does not generate bad things, nor yet good things, because he is not yet perfect; but he resembles that man who is neither sick nor yet thoroughly well, but who, after a long sickness, is at last proceeding to convalescence.

(19) What is the meaning of the statement, she had an Egyptian handmaid whose name was Hagar? (Genesis 16:1). Hagar is interpreted travelling, and she is the servant of a more perfect nature, being by nature an Egyptian less naturally; for the study of encyclical learning loves an abundance of knowledge, and abundant knowledge is, as it were, the handmaid of virtue, since the whole course and connection of sciences and arts is subservient to his use who is able to profit by their acquisition so as to attain to virtue, for virtue has the soul for its abode; but the course of arts and sciences stands in need of bodily instruments. But the body is symbolically Egypt; therefore the sacred writer here properly asserts the likeness of encyclical knowledge to Egypt. Nevertheless he has also given it a name by reason of its travelling abroad, since sophistry is a foreign thing, unconnected with the acquisition of that wisdom which alone is native, and which alone is necessary, which is the mistress of intermediate wisdom, and which conducts itself in a beautiful course through the guidance of encyclical studies.

(20) Why did Sarah say to Abraham, Behold the Lord has shut me up so that I shall not bring forth: go in now unto my handmaid so as to beget a son by her? (Genesis 16:2). In the actual letter of this statement it is the same thing to feel no envy, and also to provide for the welfare of the wise man who is her husband and her genuine brother; so that she, wishing to find a remedy for her own barrenness by means of her handmaid of whom she was mistress, gives her as a concubine to her husband. But there is a still greater abundance of her affection towards her husband indicated by this; for as she herself was accounted barren, she did not think it reasonable that the family of her husband should be left entirely without offspring, but preferred his advantage to her own dignity. This is what is indicated by this statement taken literally. But if we look to the inner sense of the passage it bears such an interpretation as this: it becomes those persons who are unable in respect of their virtue to bring forth beautiful works deserving of praise, to apply themselves to the intermediate kind of study, and, if I may so express myself, to procure themselves children from the encyclical branches of knowledge; for an abundance of knowledge is as it were the whetstone of the mind and of the intellect. And it is with great propriety that she says, The Lord has shut me up, for that which is shut up is generally opened again at a seasonable time. Therefore she was not destitute of hope, nor was her wisdom fixed in the belief that she should be for ever without offspring, but she knew that some day or other she should bring forth.

Nevertheless she will not bring forth at present, but when the soul displays the purity of its perfection. But inasmuch as it is at present imperfect it is satisfied with using a milder kind of learning, such as is attainable by encyclical studies. On which account it is not without a purpose that in the sacred contests at Olympia also, those who are unable to attain to the first prize of victory are contented to be thought worthy of the second; for there is offered to the competitors a first, and a second, and a third prize by the presidents of the games, who are representatives of nature. So now to her the sacred writer attributes the first prize of virtues, and the second prize of encyclical study.
(21) Why has he called Abraham's wife Sarah, for he says, Sarah the wife of Abraham, taking her handmaid Hagar the Egyptian, gave her into his hand? (Genesis 16:2). The sacred writer here sums up with his approbation the marriage of the good on account of those who are incontinent and lascivious; for those persons despise their wise wives for the sake of concubines, whom they love with a frantic passion: on which account he here introduces the man endued with virtue, the constant husband of one wife, at that time in which it was lawful for him to make use of her handmaid; and his wife in fact indicates that he is wise, that is to say temperate, when he enters into the bed of another woman, since his connection with his concubine was only a connection of the body for the sake of propagating children; but his union with his wife was that of two souls joined together in harmony by heavenly affection. This is the literal effect of the statement. But if we look to the inner meaning of it, then he who has truly entrusted all his secret wishes to wisdom, and justice, and the other virtues, when once he has received the counsel of wisdom, and has tasted the joys of a matrimonial connection with it, remains constant to it as the partner and companion of his life; although encyclical education would lead him in a beautiful course, since when the man eminent in virtue has become master of the sciences of geometry, and arithmetic, and grammar, and rhetoric, and the other exercises of the mind, he is not the less on that account mindful of the pursuit of honesty, but is borne on towards the one as to a necessary aim, to the other as an accessory. But it is altogether fair that that fact also should meet with our approbation, -the fact I mean of his calling his handmaid also by the name of wife, because he went up to her bed out of complacency to and at the exhortation of his real wife, and not of his own genuine inclination; on which account he no longer calls her his handmaid, that even if it were not wholly deserved still his handmaid having been given to him to wife might at least obtain the same title. But those who study allegory may be allowed to say that the exercise of the middle disciplines also stands in the place of a concubine, having nevertheless the shape and ornaments of a wife, for all encyclical learning re-produces in itself and imitates genuine virtue.
(22) What is the meaning of, "When she saw that she had conceived her mistress was despised before her?" (Genesis 16:4). The sacred writer now carefully calls Sarah the mistress when it might else have been thought that her

dignity was diminished, and that she was surpassed by her handmaid, that she, that is, who had no children, was surpassed by her who was gifted with offspring. But this kind of language is extended to nearly all the necessary affairs of human life: for a poor man who is wise is more approved of and is superior in authority to a rich man who is destitute of wisdom and reputation, or than a boasting man; and even a sick man who is wise is better than a foolish man who is well; for whatever is united with wisdom is genuine, and is endued with an authority of its own, but whatever is combined with folly is found to be slavish and inconstant. But it has been excellently said not that she despised her mistress, but that her mistress was despised; for the one statement would imply an accusation of the person, but the other contains only a declaration of an event. The scripture forsooth does not intend here to impute blame to any one while praising another, but only to hand down in an intelligible manner the pure truth of the facts. This is what is indicated by the literal statement. But if we seek the inner meaning of the words, whoever honours and embraces rank before genius and wisdom, and whoever esteems and considers the external senses of more importance than prudence and counsel, is departing from the real character of things, thinking that they have brought forth much offspring, and that having produced a great generation of visible things they are great and perfect goods, and in a singular degree noble, but that barrenness in this respect is evil, and deserving of disapprobation, because they do not see that invisible seed and that offspring which is appreciable only by the intellect, which the mind is accustomed to generate in itself and by itself.

(23) Why does Sarah as it were repent of what she has done, saying to Abraham, I am receiving injury from you: I gave my handmaid into your bosom, and now, because she sees that she has conceived, I am despised before her? (Genesis 16:5). This language indicates her anxiety and hesitation; displaying them first in the expression, "since," that is to say from the time that I gave my handmaiden, and in the second place it betokens a regard to the person of whom complaint is made, for she says, "I am receiving injury from you," a statement which in fact is a reproof, since she thinks that her husband ought always to be preserved without any stain, or any liability to blame, always virtuous and true, and in no respect forgetful of her, for she always introduces him, honouring him with all possible veneration, and calling him lord. Nevertheless, the first fact stated by her is true; for from the time that she gave her handmaiden to him to be his concubine, she herself was looked upon as despised. This is the literal meaning of her words. But if we look to their inner sense, when any one bestows on another the handmaid of wisdom, she being influenced by the counsels of sophistry, will, because she is ignorant of propriety, despise her mistress; for as she herself possesses encyclical knowledge, and is delighted with its brilliancy, where every one of the separate branches of education is by itself very attractive to the soul, as if it possesses the power of drawing it by force to itself, then she, the handmaiden, can no longer agree with her mistress, that is to say, with the image of wisdom and its glorious and admirable beauty, until that acute judge of all things, the word of God, coming in, separates and distinguishes what is probable from what is true, and the middle from the extremities, and what is second from what is placed in the first rank. On which account Sarah says, at the end of her remonstrance, "Let God judge between me and thee."

(24) Why does Abraham say, "Behold thy handmaid is in thy hand, do unto her what seems good to thee?" (Genesis 16:6). The literal expression used by the wise man contains a panegyric; for he does not call the woman who had conceived by himself, his wife, or his concubine, but the handmaiden of his wife. But since he saw that she also was a mother, he did not indulge in anger and embitter the feelings of her mind, but rather tranquillised her, and made her prudent. But the passage contains an allegory in the expression, "In thy hand:" as if, if I may so say, sophistry lives under the dominion of wisdom, which indeed does spring forth from the same fountain, but only in one part, and not directly; nor does it preserve the whole of its emanations pure, but draws up with its waters many fetid things, and many others of a similar character. Since, therefore, it is in thy hand and in thy power (for to whomsoever wisdom belongs, he is possessed also of all the branches of encyclical learning), do with it whatsoever pleases thee, for I am quite persuaded that you will judge with not more severity than justice; because that very thing is especially agreeable to you: I mean the distributing to every one according to his deserts, and giving to no one more than is just, either in the way of honouring or despising him.

(25) Why does he say, Sarah afflicted her? (Genesis 16:6). The literal meaning of the words is plain: but if we look to the inner sense of them, they contain a principle of this kind. It is not every affliction that is injurious, but there are even some occasions when they are salutary; and this is experienced by sick men at the hands of physicians, and by boys under their tutors, and by foolish people from those who correct them so as to bring them to wisdom. And this I can by no means consent to call affliction, but rather the salvation and benefit of both soul and body. Now a part of such benefit wisdom affords to the circle of encyclical knowledge; rightly admonishing the soul which is devoted to an abundance of discipline, and which is pregnant with sophism, not to rebel as if it had acquired some great and excellent good, but to acquiesce and venerate that superior and more excellent nature as its genuine mistress, in whose power is constancy itself, and authority over all things.

(26) Why did Hagar flee from her face? (Genesis 16:6). It is not every soul which is capable of proper respect and of submitting to salutary discipline, but the mind which is gentle, and good-tempered, and consistent loves reproof, and becomes more and more attached to those who correct it. But the stubborn soul becomes malignant and hates them, and turns from them, and flees away from them, preferring those discourses which are agreeable rather than those which

tend to his advantage, and looking upon them as more excellent.
(27) What is the meaning of the statement, "The angel of the Lord found her sitting by a fountain of water in the desert in the way to Sur?" (Genesis 16:7). All these statements are as it were symbols by which the sacred writer indicates that the well instructed soul, which is the possession of virtue, is nevertheless not yet able to discern the beauty of her mistress. They are, I say, symbols; I mean the statements that she was found, and that she was found by an angel in the desert, and in no other way than that leading to Sur. However we must begin with what is plain. Now the too subtle sophist and the real lover of disputations is commonly unable to be detected by reason of his artifices and sophistical persuasions, with which he is accustomed to deceive and perplex men. But he who, being free from bad habits, has only an eager desire for obtaining instruction by the course of encyclical training, although he is difficult to be detected, is yet not altogether incapable of being so; for perdition is near at hand to him who cannot be detected, but safety to him who can be discovered, especially when he is sought for and found by a more holy and more excellent spirit. And who is more holy and more excellent than the angel of the Lord? For it is to him that it has been entrusted to seek out the erring soul, the soul which, on account of its presumed erudition, is continually ignorant of her whom it ought to respect, but still she could be susceptible of correction and amendment; for which object she was sought out. Nor was she found imperfect, but ready to the hand, since the soul was found which had fled from perfect virtue, not being able to submit to discipline. But the third symbol takes place after she is found and after the discovery has been made by an angel, namely, in the fact of her being found by a fountain, that is to say, by nature; for it is nature which bestows on clever people abilities in proportion to the industry of each individual, effacing unseasonable learning, which is no learning at all: and praise is implied in the very place in which the soul is found, which is thirsting after genius and after its placid law, wishing to draw water while in the society of those who drink wine; for thus it associates with those who feed upon and are delighted with the exercise of proper training, where nature itself affords sufficient nourishment, namely, education and instruction as if from a fountain. The fourth symbol is contained in the fact that the discovery took place in the desert; since difficulty coming over each of the outward senses, together with an influx of each separate desire, represses the mind, and does not permit it to drink pure water: but when it cannot avoid these things as in the desert, it acquiesces, and, abandoning the thoughts which agitated and perplexed it, it becomes convalescent, so as to receive a hope not only of life, but even of eternal life. The fifth symbol is contained in the fact that she was found in the way; for dispositions which are incorrigible are led by devious paths; but that one which can be changed for the better, lo! It proceeds along the road which leads to virtue, and that road is like a fortified wall and guardian to the souls which are capable of being saved, for Sur means a

fortified wall. Do you not see, then, that the whole is a symbolical, or indeed a legitimate, figure of an improving soul? And, in fact, the soul which is improving does not perish as one which is wholly foolish does; for if the divine word be found by it, then again it seeks it; and he who is not pure and clean in his habits and disposition, flees from the divine word; but yet he has a fountain of water in which he washes away his vices and wickednesses, drawing from thence the fertility of the law. Besides this, it loves the desert, to which it has fled from its vices and wickednesses, and when it has once beheld the way of virtue it returns from the devious paths of wickedness. And all these things are fortified walls and bulwarks to it, so as to protect it from being ever injured by any words of circumstances which attack it, and from suffering any damage.

(28) Why did the angel say to her, "Hagar, the handmaid of Sarah, whence comest thou, and whither goest thou?" (Genesis 16:8). The plain letter of the question requires no explanation, for it is exceedingly clear; but with reference to the inner meaning contained in it, there is come asperity expressed; since the divine word is full of instruction, and is a physician of the infirmity of the soul. Therefore the angel says to her, "Whence comest thou?" knowest thou not what good thou has abandoned? Art thou not altogether lame and blind? For thou dost not see at all; and though endowed with the outward senses, dost not feel, and dost not appear to me to have any portion whatever of intellect, as if thou wert quite senseless. But "whither goest thou?" From what excellence to what misery? Why have you so erred as to cast away the blessings which you had in your power, and to pursue good things which are more remote? Do not, do not, I say, act thus; but, quitting your insane impetuosity, go back again, and return into the same way as before, looking upon wisdom as thy mistress, her whom you had before as your governess and directress in all the things which you did.

(29) What is the meaning of the answer, "I am fleeing from the face of Sarah, my mistress?" (Genesis 16:8). It is reasonable to praise a sincere disposition, and to think it friendly to truth. And moreover it is reasonable now to admit the veracity of a mind which confesses what it has suffered; for she says, "I am fleeing from the face," that is to say, I have recoiled at the outward appearance of wisdom and virtue; since, beholding its royal and imperial presence, she trembled, not being able to endure to look upon its majesty and sublimity, but rather thinking it an object of avoidance; for there are some people who do not turn from virtue from any hatred of it, but from a reverential modesty, looking upon themselves as unworthy to live with such a mistress.

(30) Why did the angel say to her, "Return to thy mistress and be humbled beneath her hands?" (Genesis 16:8). As the letter is plain, we must rather investigate its inner meaning. The word of God corrects that soul which is able to be lured, and instructs it, and converts it, leading it to wisdom as its mistress, that it may not, through being abandoned by its mistress, rush at once into absurd folly. But it warns it, not only to return to virtue, but also to be humbled beneath its hands, that is to say, beneath its several excellencies. But there are two kinds of humiliation; one, in accordance with defect, which arises from spiritual infirmity, which it is easy to overcome, seize upon, and reprove. But there is another kind which the word of the Lord enjoins, proceeding from reverence and modesty; such as that humility which children exhibit to their fathers, pupils to their masters, and young men to the aged; since it is very advantageous to be obedient, and to be subject to those who are better than one's self; for he who has learnt to be under authority is in a moment imbued with a power which he alone may exercise; for, although any one were to be clothed with the authority of all the earth and sea, yet he would not be able to possess the royal supremacy of virtue, unless he had first been instructed and taught to obey.

(31) Why did the angel say to her, "I will multiply thy seed, and it shall not be numbered for multitude?" (Genesis 16:9). It is the honour of the docile mind not to be presumptuous or rebellious on account of its progress in knowledge, or because of the very useful seed which it has received from various kinds of erudition; for it does not any more, as word catchers and cavillers do, employ all the arguments of encyclical learning to establish any whimsical object, but to prove the truth which is contained in them. And when it has begun to prosecute that by diligent investigation, it is then rendered worthy to behold the sight of its mistress, free from all acceptance of persons, and from all reproof.

(32) What is the meaning of the statement, "The angel said to her, Behold, thou hast conceived, and thou shalt bring forth a son, and shalt call his name Ishmael, because the Lord has heard the voice of thy affliction?" (Genesis 16:11). The literal sense of the words admits of no question except this allegorical explanation. Erudition, which is acquired and trained by the dispensation of virtue as a mistress, is found not to be barren, but it has conceived the seed of wisdom; and when it has conceived it brings forth; but it brings forth a work which is not perfect but imperfect, like an infant which has need of care, and ailment, and nourishment; for in truth, it is quite plain that the offspring of a perfect soul is perfect, that is to say, its words and works; but that of the soul of the second class, which is still lying in servitude and subordination, is more imperfect. On which account it has a certain name given to it, Ishmael, which is interpreted "the hearing of God." But hearing is honoured with the second dignity among the outward senses, being next to sight; for nature has arranged a succession of ranks in the contests of the senses, giving the first place to the eyes, the second to the ears, the third to the nostrils, and the fourth to that sense by which we taste.

(33) What is the meaning of the statement, "He shall be a wild man; his hand shall be upon every one, and every one's hand shall be upon him, and he shall dwell over against all his brethren?" (Genesis 16:12). If we look to the letter of the statement, up to this time Ishmael has not any brothers, for he was the first child of his parents. But the sacred writer is here figuring a certain nature, too secret to be thoroughly investigated; for he has set forth the figure of his future character. And such a figure evidently represents the sophist whose mother is erudition or wisdom. But the sophist himself is a man of wild opinions; since the wise man as being civilized is fitted for living in cities, and for urbanity, or for statesmanlike and political companionship; but he who is wild and a man of wild opinions is immediately also quarrelsome. And it is on this account that the sacred writer makes an addition, saying, "His hand shall be upon every one, and every one's hand shall be upon him;" for the abundance of science and the use of erudition is able to contradict all men. As those men of the present day who are called academicians and inquirers, consistently setting no bounds to the determinations of their will and resolution, and among the different opinions which they investigate preferring neither this nor that one, admit those men to be philosophers who attack the opinions of every sect; and those whom it has been usual to call opposers of will, as if they called them thele machoi or thele mamachoi, because they in the first place raise contentions and declare themselves the champions of their national sect, not to be convinced or put down by those who oppose them. But they are all kinsmen, and as it were brothers of the same womb, being the offspring of one mother, namely, of philosophy. And it is on this account that he says, "And he shall dwell over against all his brethren;" for in good truth the academician and the inquirer are diametrically opposed to sects, finding fault in each of them with their certain limitation of the resolution.

(34) Why does he say, "But Hagar called on the name of the Lord, who spoke to her, saying, 'Thou God who hast had regard unto me.' Because he said, 'In truth I have beheld thee appearing before me.'"(Genesis 16:13). In the first place, take notice carefully that the angel, after the manner of the handmaiden of wisdom, was a minister to her on the part of God. But still why is he here called Lord or God who ought only to have been styled his angel? It was in order to adapt the fact to the proper person; for it was right that the Lord and chief of all the universe should appear to wisdom as God, and that his word should appear as a minister to the handmaid and servant of wisdom. But we may not suppose that she mistakenly looked upon the angel as God; for those who are unable to behold the first cause may easily be deceived and look upon the second as the first; in the same manner as he who has but weak sight, not being able to behold the sun which is in heaven in its real appearance, thinks that the ray which falls upon the earth is the sun itself; and those who have never seen the king attribute frequently the dignity of the supreme sovereign to his ministers. And in truth mild and rustic men who never have beheld a city, not even from the summits of the hills where they live, think every country house or farm-yard a mighty city, and look upon the people who dwell there as citizens of a great city, out of ignorance of what a city really is.

(35) What is the meaning of, "On this account she called that well the well of him whom I have seen face to face?" (Genesis 16:14). The well has both a spring and depth. But the learning of the students of encyclical science is neither all on the surface, nor is it destitute of first principles; for it has for its source corrective discipline. Therefore it is with perfect correctness that she says that the angel appeared before the well as God; since the erudition of the encyclical training possessing the second rank is supposed to rejoice in the first authority, though it is in reality separated from that first wisdom which it is permitted to wise men to behold, but not to sophists.

(36) Why is the well said to have been between Cadesh and Pharan? (Genesis 16:14). Cadesh is interpreted holy, but Pharan is translated hail, or corn.

(37) What is the meaning of the statement, "Hagar brought forth a son to Abraham?" (Genesis 16:15). It is made in perfect accordance with nature; for no habit of possession brings forth for itself, but for him who possesses it; as grammar does for the grammarian, and music for the musician, and mathematical science for the mathematician; because it is a part of him, and stands in need of him. And the habit is not received as a thing in need of something, just as fire has no need of heat, for it is heat to itself; and it gives a portion of the participation in it to those who approach it.

(38) Why is Abraham said to have been eighty and six years old when Hagar bore Ishmael to him? (Genesis 16:16). Because the number which follows eighty, that is to say six, is the first perfect number, being equal to its parts, and being the first number which is composed of the multiplication of an odd and an even number; receiving also something from its efficient cause according to the odd or redundant number, and from its material and effective cause according to the even number. On which account, among the most ancient of our ancestors, some persons have called it matrimony, and others harmony; and our sacred historian too has divided the creation of the world into six days. But among numbers, eighty rejoices in perfect harmony, since it is composed of two generous diameters in a double and treble proportion, according to the figure of a square of four sides. And it contains within itself all the four inferences; the arithmetical, and the geometrical, and the harmonious one. Being in the first place composed of double numbers, as of six, eight, nine, twelve, the union of which makes thirty-five; in the second place of triple number, six, nine, twelve, eighteen, the sum of which amounts to forty-five. And from these two numbers thirty-five and forty-five, the whole number eighty is completed. Again, when the sacred historian Moses himself began by divine inspiration to utter the oracular precepts which he was commissioned to deliver, he was eighty years old. And the first man who existed of our nation according to the law of circumcision, being circumcised on the eighth day, being eminent for virtue, bears that name of joy, being called Isaac in the Chaldaic tongue, and Isaac means laughter; being naturally called so because nature rejoices or laughs at everything, being never vexed at any thing which is done in the world, but rather looking with complacency on every thing which occurs as being done well and profitably.

(39) Why when he was ninety and nine years old does the sacred writer say, "The Lord God appeared to him and said, I am the Lord thy God?" (Genesis 17:1). He here makes use of both the titles of each superior virtue, applying them in the case of his address to the wise man, because it was by them that all things were created, and by them that the world is regulated after it had been created. By one of them therefore the wise man, just in the same manner as the world itself, was fashioned and made according to the likeness of God; and God is the name of creative virtue; and by the other of them that he was made according to the Lord, as falling under his authority and supreme power. Therefore he designs here to show that the man who is conspicuous in virtue is both a citizen of the world, and also equal in dignity to the whole world, declaring that both the virtues of the world, the divine and the royal attributes, are in a singular manner appointed to and set over him as protectors. And it was with great correctness and propriety that this appearance took place when he was about ninety and nine years old, because that number is very near the hundred. And the number a hundred is composed of the number ten multiplied by itself, which the sacred historian calls the holy of holies. Since the first court, the first ten, is simply called holy, and that is permitted to be entered by the sweepers of the temple; but the ten of tens, which he again enjoins the sweepers of the temple to pay above all things to the existing high priest, is the number ten computed along with the number a hundred, for what else is the tenth of the tenths but the hundredth? However the number ninety and nine has been set forth and adorned not only by its affinity to the number a hundred, but it has also received a particular participation in a wonderful nature, since it consists of the number fifty, and of seven times seven. For the fiftieth year, as the year of Pentecost or the Jubilee, is called remission in the giving forth of the law, as then all things are given their liberty, whether living or inanimate. And the mystery of the seventh year is one of quiet and profound peace to both body and soul. For the seventh is the recollection of all the good things which come of their own accord without industry of labour, which at the first creation of the world nature produced of herself; but the number forty-nine, consisting as it does of seven times seven, indicates no trifling blessings, but rather those which have virtue and wisdom, in such a degree as to contribute to invincible and mighty constancy.

(40) What is the meaning of, "Do thou please me, and keep thyself from stain, and I will make my treaty between me and thee, and I will multiply thee exceedingly?" (Genesis 17:1). God here lays down a law for the human race in a somewhat familiar manner; for he who has no participation in wickedness and is free from evil, will be perfectly good, which is peculiar to incorporeal natures. But those who are in the body are called good in proportion to the measure in which wickedness and the practice of sin are removed from them. Therefore the life of those men has appeared honourable, not that of those who have been free from sickness from the beginning to the end, but that of those who from a state of infirmity have advanced to sanity; on which account he says directly and plainly, "Keep thyself free from stain," for it is sufficient to conduct a mortal nature to felicity not to be blamed, and neither to do nor say anything deserving of reproof; and such conduct is at once pleasing to the Father. Therefore it is that he said, "Do thou please me, and keep thyself free from stain." Where the form of expression implies a mutual conversion; since the habits which please God do not deserve reproof, and he who keeps himself free from stain and avoids reproof in all things is altogether pleasing to God. Therefore he promises to bestow a double blessing on him who keeps himself free from all reproof; in the first place, to make him the guardian of the deposits of the divine covenant: and in the second place to cause him to increase to a multitude without any limit. For that expression, "I will make my treaty, or covenant, between me and thee," shows the office of guardianship of the truth which is entrusted to an honest man; for the whole treaty of God is the incorporeal word; which is the form and measure of the universe according to which this world was made. And then repeating the expression, "I will multiply thee exceedingly," twice manifestly shows the immense numbers to which the multitude promised shall grow, I mean the increase which shall take place in the people, not in human virtue.

(41) What is the meaning of, "Abraham fell on his face?" (Genesis 17:3). The present expression is the interpretation of what has already been promised; for God had said, "Keep thyself free from stain," but there is not other cause of a man leading a life which is disapproved but the outward sense, because that is the origin and source of the passions; on which account he rightly and properly falls on his face, that is to say, the offences caused by the outward senses fall to the bottom, showing that the man is now devoted to all good works. This is enough to say in the first place, But in the second place we must say that he was so struck by the manifest appearance of the living God that he was scarcely able to behold him through fear, but fell to the ground and offered adoration, being overwhelmed with awe at the appearance which presented itself to him. In the third place, he fell to the ground on account of the revelation thus made to him, at the form of his appearance by the living God who exists alone, whom he knew and regarded as truth opposed to created nature, since the one exists in unvarying constancy and the other vacillates and falls into its proper place, that is to say, to the earth.

(42) What is the meaning of, "And God conversed with him, saying, And I, behold, my covenant is with thee, and thou shalt be the father of a multitude of nations?" (Genesis 17:4). Since he had previously used the expression, "treaty," he now proceeds to say, do not seek that treaty in letters, since I myself, in accordance with what has been said before, am myself the genuine and true covenant. For after he has shown himself and said, "I," he makes an addition, saying, "Behold, my covenant," which is nothing but I myself; for I am myself my covenant, according to which my treaty and agreement are made and agreed to, and according to which again all things are properly distributed and arranged. Now the form of this prototypal treating is put together from the ideas and incorporeal measures and forms in accordance with which this world was made. Is it not therefore a climax to the benefits which the Father bestowed on the wise man, to raise him up and conduct him not only from earth to heaven, nor only from heaven to the incorporeal world appreciable only by the intellect, but also to draw him up from this world to himself, showing himself to him, not as he is in himself, for that is not possible but as far as the visual organs of the beholder who beholds virtue herself as appreciable by the intellect are able to attain to. And it is on this account that he says, "Be no more a son but a father; and the father, not of one individual but of a multitude; and of a multitude, not according to a part, but of all nations;" therefore of the revealed promises two admit of a literal interpretation, but the third of one which is rather spiritual. One of those which admit of a literal interpretation is to be construed in this way: in truth thou shalt be the father of nations, and shalt beget nations, that is to say, each individual among thy sons shall be the founder of a nation. But the second is of this kind; like a father you shall be clothed with power over, and authority to rule, many nations; for a lover of God is necessarily and at once also a lover of men; so that he will diligently devote his attention, not only to his relations but also to all mankind, and especially to those who are able to go through the discipline of strict attention, and who are of a disposition the reverse of anything cruel or hard, but of one which easily submits to virtue, and willingly gives obedience to right reason. But the third we may explain under this allegory: the multitude of nations spoken of indicates as it were the multifarious inclination of the will in each of our minds, both those inclinations which it is accustomed to form with reference to itself, and also those others which it admits by the agency of the senses, as they enter clandestinely through the intervention of the imagination, and if the mind possesses the supreme authority over all these, it, like a common father, turns them to better objects, cherishing their infant opinions, as it were, with milk, exhorting those which are older and more mature, though still imperfect, to improvement, and honouring with commendation those which perform their duty aright; and again, putting a bridle, by means of discipline and reproof, on those which rebel and act rashly; since, wishing to imitate the Deity, it receives a twofold influx from the virtues of that same being, one from his beneficent attributes and another from his avenging might, as if from two sources; therefore the docile receive his kindness, and towards the rebellious he uses reproof; so that some are led to improvement by praise and others by chastisement: in truth, he who is eminent for virtue is able to be of great, and extensive, and just service to all, according to his power.

(43) What is the meaning of, "Thy name shall not be called Abram, but Abraham shall thy name be?" (Genesis 17:5). Some of those who are destitute of all knowledge of music and dancing, some indeed being wholly foolish and keeping aloof from the divine company, mock the one existing or only wise Being, immaculate by nature, saying, in a tone of vituperation, "Oh the great gift, the governor and Lord of the whole universe has given one letter, by which the name of the patriarch was to be increased and become of great importance, so as to be made a trisyllable instead of a dissyllable!" Oh the great misery, and wickedness, and impiety, of such men! If some persons dare, in any respect, to endeavour to detract from God, being deceived by the outward appearance of a name, when they ought rather to thrust their minds down into the depths, and inquire into the things themselves more closely, on account of the real magnitude and importance of the possession. Besides this, why do ye not think the concession of one letter, although a small and easy gift, nevertheless an act of providence? and why do ye not weigh its value? since, above all things, the very first element of language, as expressed in letters, is A, both in order and in virtue. In the second place, it is also a vowel, and the very first of vowels, being placed above them as their head. In the third place, because it does not belong to long properties, nor to short properties, but it is of the number of those which comprise each characteristic, for it is extended into greater length, and then again it is recalled into shortness, by reason of its softness, resembling wax, and being figured into many shapes, and afterwards figuring words, according to infinite numbers; besides all this it is a cause, for it is the brother of unity, from which all things begin and in which all things terminate. Therefore, when any one sees such great beauty, and a letter set forth with such great importance and necessity, how can he accuse it as if he had not seen this? for if he has seen it, he then shows himself to be a person of insulting disposition and a hater of what is good; and if he has not seen a fact, which is so easy to comprehend, how does he presume to ridicule and despise that which he does not understand as if he did understand it? But however these things may be said by the way, as I stated before. But we must now examine into its necessary and most important task. The addition of the letter A, by one single element, changed and reformed the whole character of the mind, causing it, instead of the sublime knowledge and learning of sublime things, that is to say, instead of astronomy, to acquire a comprehension of wisdom, since it is by the knowledge of things above that the faculty is acquired of mounting up to one portion of the world, that is to say, to heaven, and to the periodical revolutions and motions of the stars; but wisdom has reference to the nature of all things, both such as are visible to the outward senses, and such as are appreciable only by the intellect, for the intellect is the wisdom which gives a knowledge of divine and human things and of their principles. Therefore, in divine things there is something which is visible, and something else which is invisible, and a demonstrative idea. And in human affairs there are some things which are corporeal and some which are incorporeal; to attain to the right comprehension of which is a great task, and a real employment for the abilities and courage of man. But to be able, not only to behold the substances and natures of the universe, but also the principles which regulate each separate fact, indicates a virtue more perfect than that which is allotted to mankind; for it is necessary for the mind, which perceives so many and such great things, to be altogether and wholly eye, and to dispense with sleep, passing its whole existence in the world in a state of incessant wakefulness, and being surrounded by a light which knows no darkness, and which exhibits the appearance of light itself, as by an ever-flashing lightning, taking God for its leader and guide, to the comprehension of the knowledge of those things which are, and to the faculty of explaining their principles. Therefore the dissyllabic name Abram is explained as meaning "excellent father," on account of his affinity to the knowledge of sublime wisdom, that is, astronomy and mathematics. But the trisyllabic name Abraham is interpreted "the father of elect sound," being the name of a really wise man; for what else is sound in us, except the utterance of a pronounced word? for which object we have an instrument constructed by nature, passing through the thick tube of the throat, and united with the mouth and tongue; and the father of such a sound is our intellect, and elect intellect is endued with virtue. But if we are to keep to exact propriety, then it is plain that the mind is the familiar and natural father of the uttered word, because it is the especial property of the father to beget, and the word is born from the mind; and it will be a certain proof of this if we recollect that when it is set in motion by counsels it sounds, and when they are absent it ceases to sound: and the evidences of this are the rhetoricians and philosophers who demonstrate its habit by objects; for whenever the mind publishes abroad different heads of designs, and in the manner of a mother about to bring forth produces each individual means previously stored up in itself, then also the word, flowing forth like a fountain, is borne to the ears of the bystander as to its appropriate receptacles: but when those are wanting, then it also is unable to publish itself further, and rests, and the sound is inactive as being struck by no one. Now therefore, O ye men, full and crammed with superfluous loquacity, ye men devoid of wisdom, does not the gift of one single element appear to you to have been such that by the intervention of a single letter the wise man is rendered worthy of the divine attribute of wisdom, than which there is nothing more excellent in our nature? because instead of the sublime erudition of astronomy he gave him intellect, that is to say, instead of a small part of wisdom, he gave him the whole and perfect blessing of entire wisdom, since a knowledge of things above is included and comprehended in wisdom, as a part is included in the whole; for mathematics are only a part. But it becomes you, O men, to consider this point also, that the man who is well instructed and skilful in the investigation of the nature of things above may by possibility be a man of depraved and wicked habits; but the wise man is altogether approved as virtuous. Shall we then now any longer ridicule this gift, than which nothing more excellent can be found?

For what is more shameful than wickedness or more excellent than virtue? Can anything be found here not good, and is it not wholly opposed to evil? Or can this gift be compared to riches, or honour, or liberty, or health, or to any other superfluous possession of any kind around or exterior to the body? For the whole of philosophy is thus added to our life as a sort of college of medicine to the soul, in order from thence to dispense to it freedom from suffering and immunity from disease; but in truth it is noble to be a philosopher, and that wonderful knowledge is truly noble; and the end is even more admirable, on account of which the act is called into existence. Here therefore is wisdom, and that the best kind of wisdom, which God called in the Chaldaic dialect Abraham, namely the father of elect sound, giving as it were a definition of a wise man; for as the definition of man is a mortal animal endowed with reason, so also the mysterious definition of a wise man is the father of elect sound.
(44) What is the meaning of, "I will greatly increase thee, and set thee among the nations, and kings shall proceed from thee?" (Genesis 17:6). That expression, "I will greatly increase thee," was used to the wise man with exceeding propriety; since every wicked or bad man does increase and advance, not to improvement but towards deficiency, as withering flowers advance not towards life but towards death; but the man whose life is extended long and is greatly increased is like a passing cloud, or like the continually flowing stream of a river, because as it increases it is extended more and more out of doors, as its wisdom also is divine. And that expression, "I will set thee among the nations," was used in order that God might the more evidently demonstrate that he was making him worthy to be as a foundation and firm support to the nations through his wisdom, not only to his own nation, but also to all other peoples who in various manners are in want in respect of their minds, as has been said before; since the wise man is the redeemer of nations and intercessor for them before God, and since it is he who implores pardon for the sins of his relations. Last of all, the promise, "Kings shall come forth from thee," is again used with especial propriety; for everything which relates to wisdom is a royal seed; the offspring of the chief and master according to nature: but the wise man has no seed or fruit of his own, but is fertile and abundant in the seed which proceeds from the great cause himself.
(45) What is the meaning of, "I will give this land to thee and to thy seed after thee, in which thou hast sojourned, namely all the land of Canaan, for an everlasting possession?" (Genesis 17:8). The letter of the promise is so clear that the language does not stand in need of any explanation whatever; but with respect to the inward meaning of it we must have recourse to an allegory of this kind. The mind which is endowed with virtue is rather a sojourner in the corporeal space allotted to it, than a regular inhabitant of it; for its real country is the air and the heaven; and the earth, and the earthly body in which it is said to sojourn, is only a colony; therefore the Father, conferring a benefit upon it, gives to it the sovereign authority over all the things of the earth for ever and

ever, as he says himself, for an everlasting possession; so that it for the future shall not be governed by the body, but shall always be its master and ruler, having the body for its servant and attendant.

(46) What is the meaning of, "And every male of you shall be circumcised, and you shall circumcise, or you shall be circumcised, in, the flesh of your foreskin?" (Genesis 17:10). I see here a twofold circumcision, one of the male creature, and the other of the flesh; that which is of the flesh takes place in the genitals, but that which is of the male creature takes place, as it seems to me, in respect of his thoughts. Since that which is, properly speaking, masculine in us is the intellect, the superfluous shoots of which it is necessary to prune away and to cast off, so that it, becoming clean and pure from all wickedness and vile, may worship God as his priest. This therefore is what is designated by the second circumcision, where God says by an express law, "Circumcise the hardness of your hearts," that is to say, your hard and rebellious thoughts and ambition, which when they are cut away and removed from you, your most important part will be rendered free.

(47) Why orders he the males only to be circumcised? (Genesis 17:11). For in the first place, the Egyptians, in accordance with the national customs of their country, in the fourteenth year of their age, when the male begins to have the power of propagating his species, and when the female arrives at the age of puberty, circumcise both bride and bridegroom. But the divine legislator appoints circumcision to take place in the case of the male alone for many reasons: the first of which is, that the male creature feels venereal pleasures and desires matrimonial connexions more than the female, on which account the female is properly omitted here, while he checks the superfluous impetuosity of the male by the sign of circumcision. But the second reason is, that the material of the female is supplied to the son from what remains over of the eruption of blood, while the immediate maker and cause of the son is the male. Because therefore the male supplies the most indispensable part in the fact of generation, God deservedly represses his pride by the figure of circumcision, but the material or feminine cause, as being inactive, does not display ambition in the same degree. And this is enough to say on this head. But afterwards we must note this likewise, that the intellect in us is endued with the power of sight, therefore it is necessary to cut away its superfluous shoots. And these superfluous shoots are empty opinions, and all the actions which are done in accordance with them. So that the intellect after circumcision may only bear about with itself what is necessary and useful; and that whatever causes pride to increase may be cut away; with which also the eyes are circumcised as if they did not see.

(48) Why did he say, "And let the child, every male child, be circumcised at eight days old?" (Genesis 17:12). He orders the freeborn to be circumcised, which, in the first place, was permitted on account of diseases that might arise; for it is more difficult to heal a disease in the genitals, and it is commonly done by burning by fire those parts over which a membrane grows, but this rarely affects those who have been circumcised. And in truth, if it were possible that other infirmities also could be avoided by amputating any member or any part of the body, so that though it was amputated still the operation of each necessary part would not be hindered, then without the knowledge of mortal man he would be transmitted into immortality. But that here it was thought fit that man should be circumcised out of a provident care for his mind without any previous infirmity is plain, since not the Jews alone, but also the Egyptians, and Arabians, and Ethiopians, and nearly all the nations who live in the southern parts of the world, down to the torrid zone are circumcised. What then is the chief reason of this fact? except that in those districts, and especially in the summer, when the genitals are protected with a skin, it burns and is injured by inflammation, but when that covering is laid bare by circumcision it is cooled, and the disease is repelled; and on this account the northern nations and others, to whom the cooler portion of the habitable earth has been allotted, are not circumcised, for not only is the solar heat moderate in those regions, but so is also all inflammatory disease which affects the membranes of the members. Let every one take a firm judgment, and from that time when the disease comes in more vigorously; for it never comes at all in the winter, but in the summer it shows itself and flourishes and ripens; for it loves, if I may so say, like fire to burn in those parts. In the second place, it was not only from a regard to sound health that our ancestors diligently employed this method of cure, but also from a regard to the multiplication of the human race, seeing that nature was very vivacious and too eager to propagate the human species. Therefore they knew, like wise men, how the seed when poured over the folds of the membrane is often accustomed to be wasted and so to become unfruitful; but if no impediment arises then it would easily be able to arrive at the situation suited to receive it. On which account also those nations which adopt the practice of circumcision have grown into an exceedingly numerous population: and our legislator, weighing the consequences also, commanded the circumcision of infants to be performed at an earlier age, keeping in view the same effect of circumcision with regard to the population. Therefore it is in truth, as it seems to me, that the Egyptians also in the fourteenth year of their children's age, in which the desire to propagate the species usually begins, have said that it is suitable to circumcise them, with the view of increasing the population; but it was better and more carefully done in our nation, where the circumcision of infants was ordained, since perhaps the man when grown up would delay the operation out of fear, because he then has a will of his own. In the third place, he says this with a view to cleanliness in the sacred oblations; for in truth those who enter into the courts of the temples are made clean by sprinkling and ablutions. Moreover the Egyptians scrape the whole body, removing all the hairs which cover and envelop the body, so as to appear white all over; but the circumcision of the skin is no small assistance towards cleanliness, otherwise everyone would abhor it when he beheld it as it is in itself. In the fourth place, there are in us two generative principles, one in the soul and one in the body; the generative principle of the soul is the intellect, and that of the body is the corporeal organ; therefore the ancients chose to refer the generative principle of the body to an imitation of the intellect which is rather the generative principle of the heart. And in truth there is nothing to which it is found more like than the circumcision of the heart; these therefore are real facts like the celebrated reasons for things which have been investigated. But we must now speak of those which have greater symbols belonging to them and which exhibit a certain principle. Therefore the circumcision of the skin is said to be a symbol, but as one indicating that it is proper to cut away all superfluous and extravagant desires, by studying continence and religion; for as the skin of the prepuce is quite superfluous for generation, and is moreover especially injurious by reason of the disease of inflammation which burns within it, so also an over abundance of desire is as superfluous as it is pernicious, superfluous because it is not necessary, and pernicious because it is the cause of diseases to both body and soul; and by the greater desire he also warns us that all the other desires are likewise to be cut off. And that is called the greater desire which has a regard to the matrimonial connexion of the male and the female; since it is the beginning of a great thing, namely, of generation; and since it creates a great affection on the part of the father towards her who is to bring forth; for it is natural for them both to be influenced by love and affection for their offspring. Therefore, he here warns us to cut away not only all the superfluous desires, but also pride, as being a great wickedness and an associate of wickedness. For pride, as the language of the ancients tells us, is what keeps men back and hinders them in their improvement; since it will not exhibit that honesty which it really possesses, thinking that it is itself an adequate cause for anything. Moreover it naturally influences those who think themselves the causes of generation; so that they scarcely ever turn their minds at all to behold the true Father of the universe. For he is in truth the one real and genuine Father of all; and we, who are called fathers, are only instruments of his, serving to generation; since, as in a wonderful resemblance, all things which are represented in appearance are yet in reality inanimate, but that which strengthens the nerves is invisible, and yet is itself the cause of virtue, and of motion, and of sight. So, in like manner, from everlasting and invisible space there extends the Creator of the universe, and we, like so many puppets, are strengthened by him with nerves for the purpose which belongs to us, namely, sowing seed and raising a generation; unless we choose to fancy that a flute is blown by itself, and is not made by an artist in a way adapted for the production of harmony, by whom it was constructed as an instrument for service and for its own necessary end.

(49) Why does he order circumcision to be performed on the eighth day? (Genesis 17:12). The number eight has many beauties in it; for it is, in the first place, a cubic number. Secondly, it has beauties, because it everywhere contains in itself the form of equality, because longitude, and breadth, and depth, which are all equal to one another, are indicated by the first number eight. In the third place, the composition of the number eight produces agreement, namely, the number thirty-six, which the Pythagoreans call agreement, since that is the first number in which odd numbers being added together agree with even numbers. If, indeed, four odd numbers from the unit are separately taken and added together and four even numbers beginning with two, they united make thirty-six. Now the odd numbers are these: one, three, five, seven, which make sixteen. And the even numbers are these: two, four, six, eight, which make twenty. And the addition of the two together makes thirty-six, which is in truth a more fertile number. Since it is a square, having each side composed of the number six; the first of which is both odd and even; which some persons most correctly call harmony or matrimony; and it was by the employment of this number that the Creator of the universe made the world, as the holy and admirable book of Moses relates. In the fourth place, the idea of eight produces sixty-four, which is the first number, which is a cube and also a square, being the type of incorporeal substance appreciable only by the intellect and invisible, and also of corporeal substance. Of incorporeal substance, inasmuch as it produces superficies according to the square; and of corporeal substance, as producing a solid according to the cube. In the fifth place, it is always a kindred number to the virgin number seven, for seven makes up the parts of eight; because four is the half of it, two is the fourth part of it, one the eighth of it, and four, two, and one, added together, make seven. In the sixth place, the power of eight is sixty-four, which we call the first number, being both a cube and a square. In the seventh place, taken separately from the units by these doubled numbers, one, two, four, eight, sixteen, thirty-two, the sum makes sixtyfour. And the number eight has also other more distinguished virtues still, which we have enumerated in another place; but now it seems better to explain the principle which corresponds to the present question, and which depends on the grounds now laid down. But in the first place we must premise this: that nation to whom it is enjoined, having the commandments give to it, that it should be circumcised on the eighth day, is called in the Chaldaic language Israel, that is to say, "he that seeth by day." Therefore God wills, in the first place, that he should be a partaker both of his own just rights, and also of those which exist according to election, and according to the principle of Genesis (or creation), by that first number six, which immediately followed the creation. This number, in fact, the Father and Creator of all things evidently exhibited to the world as the festival of generation, completing the world on the sixth day. And the other number, that which is according to election, he exhibited by the number eight, which is the beginning of the second seven; as eight is seven and one, so the race which has been honoured is always a race receiving that number also in addition, so that it should be elect, both by nature and in accordance with the decree of the Father. In the second place, the number eight exhibits equality everywhere, showing that all its separations are equal, as has been already said, I mean its length, and breadth, and depth. And equality it is which is the parent of equity and justice, by which he shows that the nation which loves God is adorned with equity or justice, and has advanced to complete possession. In the third place, eight is not only a measure of complete equity in all its dimensions, but is the very first number that is so, for it is the first cube; since the number eight indicates equality, and so it has the second and not the first rank: therefore it demonstrates in a symbolical manner that that nature was the first which was ever completely furnished with consummate and perfect equity and justice, and that it is the first nature of the human race, not in point of creation or of time, but in the dignity of virtue, as if justice united with equality were a connatural part of it. In the fourth place, since there are four elements, the appearances of earth, water, air, and fire; fire has received for its figure a shape becoming a similar name, a pyramid; {4}{pyramis, resembling the word pyr, "fire."} and air has received for its figure an eight-sided one; water, a twenty-sided one; and the earth, a cube. Therefore he thought it necessary that the earth, which was to be the allotment of the race of man, who were endowed with virtue, should participate in the cubic number, as the whole earth has been formed in its figure. And a part of it receives the parts of that which should bring forth, because by nature the earth is very fertile, producing all the various and distinct species of every kind of animal and plant.

(50) Why does he order all slaves to be circumcised, those born in the family and also those who are bought? (Genesis 17:12). The literal meaning is plain; for it is fitting that servants should imitate their masters on account of their necessary employment, and the services to which they are bound in life. But with respect to the inner object of the command, those dispositions are what may be called born in the family which are influenced by nature itself, and those are bought which can be changed for the better by teaching and instruction. Each of these has its appropriate employment, and requires like a plant to be cleared and pruned in order that the good and fruitful parts may acquire constancy; for fertile plants produce many superfluous things by reason of their fecundity, and those superfluities must be cut away; but those who are taught by instructors cut away their ignorance.

(51) What is the meaning of, "And it shall be my covenant (or agreement) in your flesh?" (Genesis 17:13). God is willing to do good, not only to the man who is endued with virtue, but he wishes that the divine word should regulate not only his soul but his body also, as if it had become its physician. And it must be its care to prune away all excesses of seeing, and hearing, and taste, and smell, and touch, and also those of the instrument of voice and articulation, and also all the redundant and pernicious impulses of the genitals, as also of the whole body, the effect of which is, that at times we are delighted by our passions and at times pained by them.

(52) Why is it that he pronounces a sentence of death on an infant, saying, "Every male child who is not circumcised, who has not been circumcised (or, as the Greek has it, who shall not be circumcised) in the flesh of his foreskin on the eighth day, that soul shall be cut off from his generation?" (Genesis 17:14). The law never declares a man guilty for any unintentional offence; since even those who have committed an unintentional homicide are pardoned by it, cities being set apart into which such men may flee and there find security; for whoever escapes to them is rendered secure and free from danger; and no one has the power to drag him forth, or to cite him before the tribunal of the judge for the deed. Therefore, if a boy is not circumcised on the eighth day after his birth, what offence will he have committed that he is to be held guilty, and suffer the penalty of death? Some persons may perhaps say that the form of the command points to the parents themselves, for they look upon them as despisers of the command of the law. But others say that it has here exerted excessive severity against infants, as it seems, imposing this heavy penalty in order that grown up persons who break the law may thus be irrevocably subjected to most severe punishment. This is the literal effect of the words. But if we look to their inward meaning, then what is male in us is most especially the intellect, and that God here commands to be circumcised on the eighth day, for the reason previously stated, not in any other part, but in the flesh of the foreskin, by this expression symbolically indicating those parts which in the flesh do subsequently become the organs of pleasure and impulse. And on this account it is that he introduces a legitimate reason, warning men that the intellect, which is not circumcised and cleared away from the flesh and the vices of the flesh, is corrupt and cannot be saved. But that this language is not to be applied to the man, but to the intellect, which is thus put in a sound condition, he tells us in the subsequent words, saying, "that soul shall be cut off," not that human body, or that man, but that soul and mind. Cut off from what? From its generation; for the whole generation is incorrupt. Therefore the wicked man is removed from incorruption to corruption.

(53) Why does God say, "Sara thy wife shall not be called Sara, but Sarra shall be her name?" (Genesis 17:15). Here again some foolish persons may laugh at the addition of one single letter, that is to say, of a hundred, for in Greek characters the letter r means a hundred; but if they jest in this way they are foolish, as being unwilling to behold the inward merits of things and to cleave to the footsteps of truth; for that element, r, which is here thought of merely as the addition of one letter, is the parent of all harmony, making things great instead of small, general instead of particular, and mortal instead of immortal; since Sara, when called Sara with one r, is interpreted "thy princedom," but with two r's, Sarra, "princess." Let us then be careful, and see how these two names are distinguished from one another. In me wisdom (or prudence), integrity (or temperance), justice, and fortitude have only a prince-like power and are mortal; moreover, when I die they die too. But this wisdom is herself a princess, and justice is a prince too, and each separate one of these virtues is not the principal or princely part in me, but is itself a mistress and a queen, an everlasting monarchy and sovereignty. Do you not now see the magnitude of the gift? By this slight change, God changes the part into the whole, the species into the genus, the corruptible into the incorruptible. And all these things are previously dispensed on account of the impending birth of a more perfect joy than all joys, whose name is Isaac.

(54) Why does he say, "And from her I will give thee children, and I will bless him, and he shall be over the nations, and kings of the nations shall come forth from him?" (Genesis 17:16). It is scarcely proper to inquire why he has said children in the plural number, when he meant their only and beloved son; for the intention of God's words applies to his offspring, from which nations and kings should arise. This is the literal meaning of the words. But if we look to their more inward sense, when the soul possesses that virtue, small and mortal as it is, which is only particular, she is still barren. But from the time that it acquires a share of the divine and incorruptible virtue, it begins to conceive and to bring forth varieties of nations, namely, of all other holy and sacred persons; for ever one of the everlasting virtues is subject to an immense number of voluntary laws, which bear in themselves a similarity to nations and kingdoms; for virtue and the generations of virtue are royal things, being previously instructed by nature what it is which rejoices in princely power, and has no knowledge of a servile condition.

(55) Why did Abraham fall on his face and laugh? (Genesis 17:17). Two things are indicated by his falling on his face. One an act of adoration on account of the excess of his divine ecstacy; the other that it corresponds to and is suitable to the aforesaid harmony, by which the intellect has confessed that God alone exists in a continual and unvarying existence. But those creatures which owe their existence to creation and generation, all are subject to changes in time; for they fall to a certain extent, inasmuch as they are accustomed to rise up, and to be corrected in accordance with their original appearance. And it was very natural for Abraham to laugh at the promise, as he was then filled with the great hope that the things which he expected should be accomplished, especially because he had received a manifest revelation from that appearance, by which he became more thoroughly acquainted with him who exists for everlasting without variation, and with him also who is continually stooping and falling.

(56) Why did Abraham appear to hesitate about the promise, for the sacred writer says, He said in his mind, shall there be a son to one who is a hundred years old; and shall Sarra, who is ninety years old, bring forth a child? (Genesis 22:18). This expression, "he said in his mind," is not added without an object or gratuitously, for words which are articulated in the tongue and the mouth incur guilt, and become liable to punishment, but those which are restrained within the mind are not liable to punishment, because the mind without any intention on its part is led away by irregularities, all kinds of passions being introduced from different quarters, which it for a while resists, being indignant at them, and wishing to keep aloof from their representations. But perhaps we should not say that he hesitated, but rather that he was struck by wonderment at the amazing nature of the gift, and so said, "Behold my body is advanced in years, and has passed the age of generation; nevertheless all things are possible to God, so that he may transmute old age into youth, and lead those who have no seed nor fruit to fertility and generation: and if a man who is a hundred years and a woman who is ninety years old become parents, all commonplace occurrences and all regularity of nature will be done away, and it will be clearly seen that it is only the power and the grace of God." But what virtue the number one hundred has must now be explained. In the first place, a hundred is the power of the number ten. In the second place, the number ten thousand is the power of this number a hundred, and ten thousand is the brother of the unit, for as one times one is one, so ten thousand times one is ten thousand. In the third place, every part of the number a hundred is honourable. In the fourth place, this number consists of thirty-six and sixty-four, which is a cube, and at the same time a triangle. In the fifth place, it is composed of all these separate odd numbers: one, three, five, seven, nine, eleven, thirteen, fifteen, seventeen, nineteen, which added together make a hundred. In the sixth place, it is composed of these four numbers: one and its double, and four and its double; as one, two, four, eight, which make fifteen, and of these four numbers also added together, one, four, fifteen, sixty-four, which make eighty-five And the principle of doubling pervades all these numbers, containing that principle which is by fours and by fives: and the principle of four times and twice pervades them all. In the seventh place, it is composed of five numbers taken simply, one, two, three, four, which make ten; and of five triangular numbers, one, three, six ten, which make twenty; and of five quadrangular numbers, one, four, nine, sixteen, which make thirty; and of five quinquangular numbers, one, five, twelve, twenty-two, which make forty: and all these added together make a hundred. In the eighth place, it is composed of four cubes taken simply beginning with the unit, for after giving one, two, three, four, their cubes one, eight, twenty-seven, sixty-four, make a hundred. In the ninth place, it is divided into forty and sixty, each of which is a very natural number; and in accordance with the first order of decimals up to ten thousand in a quinquangular figure the number a hundred holds the middle place; for instance: one, ten, a hundred, one thousand, ten thousand, where a hundred is the middle number of one, ten, a hundred, one thousand, and ten thousand. But we ought also not to pass over in silence the number ninety as far as it concerns the visible characters. As it seems to me the number ninety is second only to the number a hundred, inasmuch as the tenth part of it, that is to say ten, is taken away, since I see that in the law two-tenths of the firstfruits were set apart, first a tenth of the whole, secondly a tenth of the remainder, for when a tenth of the fruits of the earth, of corn, or wine, or oil, is taken, another tenth is also taken from the remainder; therefore of these two that which is the first and principal one is honoured with the greater share; and in the second place that which follows it, since the number a hundred of the years of the wise man comprises both the first-fruits with which it is consecrated, both the first and the second kind; but the number ninety of the years of the female parent, comprehends the second and lesser first-fruits, namely, the remainder of the first, which is the great one among the sacred numbers. This therefore may be called the first vision in the sacred law which is familiar; and the other has a general character, for the number ninety is fertile; on which account also it happens that the woman begins to bring forth in the ninth month; but the tenth is the sacred and perfect number; and when the two numbers nine and ten are multiplied together ninety is made, as being the virtue of the sacred birth, receiving a fertile generation according to the number nine, and a holy one according to ten.

(57) Why did Abraham say to God, O may this my son Ishmael live before thee? (Genesis 17:18). In the first place, I do not despair, says he, O Lord, of a better generation, but I believe thy promise: nevertheless, it would be a sufficient blessing for me for this son to live who in the meantime is a living son, standing visibly, even though he be not so according to the legitimate blood, but is only born of a concubine. In the second place, that blessing which he is now asking for is an additional one; for he does not entreat for life alone for his sons, but for an especial life in God; and we must suppose that there is nothing more perfect than the rejoicing in the presence of God with a salutary soundness of mind, which is equal to immortality. In the third place, he by a conjecture intimates that the divine law, when heard, ought not to be considered enough if merely heard, but that it ought also to enter more deeply into the inward man, and to form his principal part; for that life is worthy of being beheld by the Deity which is formed in accordance with his word.

(58) Why does the divine oracle, in the way of intimation, say to Abraham, Yes, be it so: behold Sarah thy wife shall also bring forth a son unto thee? (Genesis 17:19). The meaning of this sentence is as follows: that confession and admission, says God, is on my part an admission of thy wish, being manifestly full of unadulterated joy; and your faith is not doubtful, but without any hesitation it has a share of modest awe and reverence; therefore that which thou hast received before, as to be done unto thee on account of thy faith in me, shall certainly be done; for this is what is meant by yes.

(59) Why does he say, But behold I will also listen to thee concerning Ishmael, and I will bless him, and he shall become the father of twelve nations? (Genesis 17:20). God says, I will grant to thee both the first and the second blessing, that is to say, both the blessings of nature and the blessings of instruction; by nature that which is according to the legitimate course of nature, that is Isaac, and by instruction that which is according to Ishmael, who is not legitimate: for hearing, when compared with sight, is like the illegitimate compared with the legitimate, and what is brought about by instruction is not of the same class with that which owes its existence to nature; and the man who is desirous of encyclical wisdom becomes the father of nations, for the encyclical number is a period of twelve days and years.

(60) Why does he say, But I will set up my covenant with Isaac, whom Sarah shall bring forth about this time in the succeeding year? (Genesis 17:21). As in men's wills some persons are set down as heirs, and some are entered as worthy of gifts which they are to receive from the heirs, so also in the divine testament that man is set down as the heir who is by nature a worthy disciple of God being adorned with all perfect virtues; but he who is introduced by learning, and is made subject to the law of wisdom, and partakes in encyclical instruction, is not at all an heir, but only a receiver of gifts gratuitously given. But it is said with great wisdom and propriety that his mother shall bring forth Isaac in the succeeding year, since this birth unto life does not belong to the present time, but to another great and holy time; and that which is divine rejoices in excessive abundance, and is by no means like the nations of this world.

(61) Why does he say, Abraham was ninety and nine years old when he was circumcised, and Ishmael his son was thirteen years old? (Genesis 17:24). The number of ninety and nine years is arranged here as approximating to the number a hundred. And it is in accordance with this number that it is arranged that the seed of the perfect man becomes the beginning of generation, which appears more evidently in the number a hundred; but the number thirteen is composed of the first square numbers of four and nine, the odd and even numbers; so that the even number has for its sides a twofold material form; and the odd number has an operative form, from all which a triple number is made, which is the greatest and most perfect of the festival victims which the examinations of the sacred scriptures contain. This is one reason. A second also it may be allowed to us to mention, that the age namely of thirteen years is very near to and a partaker with the fourteenth year, in which the motions of seed towards generation begin to have life. In order, therefore, that no foreign seed should be sown, he arranged that the first generations should be kept pure, figuring the instrument of generating under the figure of generation. In the third place, he teaches that he who is about to go through the operations of matrimony ought by all means first of all to cut away concupiscence, reproving all lascivious and effeminate persons as those who bring together superfluous mixtures which were not for the sake of the generation of children but to gratify incontinent desires.

(62) Why did Abraham also circumcise strangers? (Genesis 17:27). The wise man is as useful as the humane man, who saves and invites to himself not only his relations and neighbours, but also strangers and men of another family, giving them a share of his own habit of patient and religious continence; for these are the foundations of constancy, which is the object of all virtue, and the point at which it rests.

www.ingramcontent.com/pod-product-compliance
Ingram Content Group UK Ltd.
Pitfield, Milton Keynes, MK11 3LW, UK
UKHW040601210726
13854UKWH00008B/1665

9 780244 194833